PRAISE FOR
PREACHING AND STEWARDSHIP

"Craig Satterlee writes the preaching books the church needs. *Preaching and Stewardship* will come as a joyful surprise to preachers who have been bogged down for years trying to say stewardship is about everything but money. Satterlee puts the 'M' word front and center without losing sight of a heartfelt theological vision for Christian community."
—*John A. Dally, Garrett-Evangelical Theological Seminary*

"Satterlee's volume on preaching and stewardship demonstrates a wonderfully direct and unapologetic approach to a topic many church leaders lament addressing. This book is an invaluable guide for preachers who long to believe that biblically grounded and clearly articulated sermons on stewardship can grow people's giving and their faith."
—*Stephen Chapin Garner, author,* Getting Into Character: The Art of First-Person Narrative Preaching

"This is definitely not just another book on stewardship sermons! Craig Satterlee unapologetically addresses preaching about giving money to the church in response to the gospel and does so with keen biblical and theological insight. The book is forthright and helpful to preachers timid about mentioning money in a sermon."
—*Rev. Ann I. Hoch, pastor, Memorial Presbyterian Church, Fredericksburg, Texas*

"At last! A book on preaching and stewardship that is both full of good, practical sense and replete with soaring theology. Satterlee shakes us loose from all mundane notions of stewardship in favor of the claim that the way we use money can be a bold 'act of resistance to the powers at work in the world that are opposed to God.' Many preachers dread the annual stewardship sermon, but Satterlee ably shows how 'messing with mammon' can be a prophetic, exciting task for the preacher."
—*Thomas G. Long, Bandy Professor of Preaching, Candler School of Theology, Emory University, Atlanta, GA*

"Centered in Gospel grace, this book will inspire stewardship preaching grounded in the abundant generosity of God. Anecdotes, sample sermons, and leading questions provide practical resources for crafting faithful sermons about the often awkward topic of money and God."
—*Marty E. Stevens, Associate Professor of Biblical Studies and Stewardship in the Arthur L. Larson position of Stewardship and Parish Ministry at Lutheran Theological Seminary at Gettysburg*

Preaching and Stewardship

Preaching and Stewardship

PROCLAIMING GOD'S INVITATION TO GROW

CRAIG A. SATTERLEE

ALBAN

Herndon, Virginia
www.alban.org

The Alban Institute
2121 Cooperative Way, Suite 100
Herndon, VA 20171

Unless otherwise noted, all Scripture quotations are from the New Revised Standard Version of the Bible, © 1989, Division of Christian Education of the National Council of Churches of Christ in the United States of America, and are used by permission.

Cover design by Tobias Becker, Bird Box Design

Author photo by Daniel W. Hille

Library of Congress Cataloging-in-Publication Data

Satterlee, Craig Alan, 1959-
  Preaching and stewardship : proclaiming God's invitation to grow / Craig A. Satterlee.
      p. cm.
  Includes bibliographical references (p. 171).
  ISBN 978-1-56699-417-0
  1. Christian giving. 2. Topical preaching. 1. Title.
  BV772.S325 2011
  248'.6--dc23
                    2011020931

11   12   13   14   15   VP   5   4   3   2   1

In loving memory of
Connie M. Kleingartner
Colleague, Collaborator, Coconspirator, Comrade,
Child of God
I miss you.

Contents

Preface

EARLY IN 2007, MY FRIEND Connie Kleingartner, de facto director of the Tithing and Stewardship Foundation at the Lutheran School of Theology at Chicago, *informed* me that I would deliver the keynote address at a conference on preaching and stewardship that April. "I don't know anything about preaching and stewardship," I responded. "Sure you do," Connie replied. "No, Connie, I don't," I said. "Then I guess you'll learn," Connie responded smiling. "The conference is in April. You'll be great." So I learned. I reread the books and reviewed my notes from a stewardship course I took in seminary twenty years earlier—thanks, Paul Fransen. More important, I talked to preachers, particularly my friend Tim Olson, students in the ACTS Doctor of Ministry in Preaching Program, and, of course, Connie.

The lecture went well, and the topic would not let go of me. Seminarians in my advanced homiletics seminars wanted to talk about preaching and stewardship; preachers at continuing education events wanted to as well. I continued to learn. I continued to read. I continued to talk to preachers and congregational leaders about preaching, money, and giving. My thinking evolved. Connie told me I needed to write it down. She said the church needed a book about preaching and stewardship, since one was long overdue. Thankfully, my partners at the Alban Institute agreed.

Connie did not live long enough to see this book, or even the article I wrote for the Tithing and Stewardship Foundation, which summarized my lecture and provided the book's outline.[1] The last time Connie and I had coffee together, she *informed* me that I was going to write this book. I promised her that I would, and we cried that she would not see it. While I cannot say whether a book about preaching and stewardship is behind schedule in the life of the church, I do know that I am long overdue in keeping this promise to my friend.

Another thing I know for sure about preaching and stewardship, which I never told Connie, is that for a long time, the annual stewardship sermon scared me to death. To me, it seemed that the congregation's future was at stake and that everything hinged on that single sermon. As I spoke with other preachers, I learned that I am not alone; they too were intimidated by this preaching task. Perhaps you are feeling overwhelmed or a bit afraid because the annual stewardship sermon is just a few weeks away. My aim in writing this book is to help preachers like me—and perhaps you—think about and prepare that sermon. While definitions of *stewardship* have expanded from "money for the church" to "time, talent, and treasure" to a leadership philosophy to care of the planet to an all-encompassing catchphrase that summarizes everyone's passion and project, this book is confined to preaching about money and giving to the church. If you have some other definition of stewardship in mind, such as getting people to volunteer or recycle, you might approach this book as a case study.

I organized this book around some questions preachers ought to ask themselves as they prepare the stewardship sermon. In chapter 1, I ask, "What do you mean by *stewardship*?" In other words, what is the topic of the sermon? Whatever it is, I advise using that word instead of *stewardship*. Since my topic is money and giving, I discuss six truths of giving to the church that shape preaching about money in important ways. In chapter 2, I ask, "Why should I give to the church?" I argue that the way preachers answer this question from the pulpit says something about who God is, whether we are aware of it or not. I then answer, "Since the primary purpose of preaching is to proclaim the gospel, when we preach about stewardship, we ask people to give to the church in response to the gospel." I then offer possibilities, limitations, and implications for preaching about money and giving in response to the gospel that affect the purpose, subject, approach, and structure of the stewardship sermon.

In chapters 3 through 6, I consider the exegetical part of preparing the stewardship sermon. In chapter 3, I ask, "What does the Bible say?"

and offer guidelines that govern how preachers select and interpret Scripture for the stewardship sermon. In chapter 4, I ask, "Why does the Bible say we give?" I provide six reasons Scripture suggests for giving to God in response to the gospel. In chapter 5, I ask, "How does the Bible say we are to give?" Here I encourage preachers to allow Scripture to determine the tone, or spirit, of the stewardship sermon. Because one way the Bible says people of faith are to give is intentionally, in chapter 6, I ask, "How much does the Bible tell us to give?" and describe biblical plans for giving.

Turning from preparing the stewardship sermon to preaching it, I ask, "Why is this sermon so hard?" In chapter 7, I name some of the assumptions preachers and congregations bring with them to worship, which make it difficult to preach and hear the stewardship sermon. I know at some level many preachers and congregational leaders dare to hope the stewardship sermon will transform lives or at least produce needed income for the church; therefore, I include a historical assessment of preaching about money and giving in this chapter. In chapter 8, I acknowledge the stewardship sermon cannot do the job all by itself and ask, "What else can we do?" I am particularly interested in strengthening the offering as an act of worship and including testimony in the service. I conclude each chapter with questions that I hope will assist you as you prepare to preach or hear the stewardship sermon.

If you are steeped in stewardship literature, you are not likely to find anything revolutionary here, except perhaps the way I put the pieces together. Those familiar with my work will find well-worn themes, including "preach the gospel," along with some of my favorite quotes from colleagues in the field of homiletics. I certainly do not say everything that can be said about preaching, money, and giving. In fact, if something someone wrote does not ring true to me as a preacher, I do not include it in this book.

This book is loaded with Scripture; however, I do not consider myself a biblical scholar and so do not presume to provide detailed exegesis of biblical texts. As I have said elsewhere, I believe that in baptism, God draws us into the biblical story of salvation. As Christians and as a church, we understand ourselves in biblical terms, and we experience, perceive, and evaluate our lives and the world using the language of the Bible. We therefore consciously cultivate the characters, images, and stories of the Bible as the way we frame our lives and the world.[2] I have undertaken to do this in the pages that follow by writing in the mother tongue of the Christian faith, the language of Scripture. As the Christian community becomes increasingly fluent in the language of Scripture, we hear God speaking in the voices around us and even in our own. This is what Peter did at Pentecost—connected the sounds of the rush of violent wind with the words of the prophet Joel, and the story of Jesus with words attributed to David (Acts 2:1–36). Imagine how giving might change if we talked about our weekly offerings in terms of Elijah and the widow of Zarephath (1 Kings 17:8–16) instead of as a profit and loss statement.

Connie was adamant that this book should include sermons; she hoped for an entire collection. I understand sermons as events in time and space rather than manuscripts. Elsewhere, I have written readily about the challenges of translating sermons edited for publication into authentic preaching.[3] Published sermons lose their voice, and sermon manuscripts can be scrutinized to a degree that preached sermons cannot. Sometimes the rewards outweigh the challenges. Amid the hundreds of sermons I heard in the past few years, a handful of stewardship sermons stick with me. When I felt that one of these sermons truly illustrated a point I was making, I included it. I am grateful to Kirsten L. Fryer, Donald P. Kreiss, and Seth Moland-Kovash for entrusting me with their sermons so that I might share them with you. Except for minor editing, I present these sermons as they were preached and have not undertaken to perfect or idealize them, with the result that I share a sermon that was never preached or heard.

I acknowledge the Lutheran School of Theology at Chicago for providing me a sabbatical leave to write this book. I am grateful to Emily Carson, Gretchen Freese, Timothy V. Olson, and Jennifer Phelps Ollikainen for reading early drafts of chapters. Barry Hopkins assisted with research, Clark Kristofor Olson-Smith compiled the appendix, and Anna Ballan proofread the final manuscript. It has been a few years since I worked with my editor and friend, Beth Gaede, and I was delighted to discover anew what joy and grace that collaboration brings me. I am thankful for the wonderful way Andrea Lee spruces up my work for you. As my wife, Cathy, has done for twenty years, she blessed, sustained, and enriched me in ways that make writing—and living—possible.

Yet, the real grace in writing this book was inviting our daughter Chelsey home for Christmas during her first year at the University of Michigan to read and edit the manuscript. Chelsey's "fingerprints" are all over these pages, and this book is better because they are. In particular, Chelsey challenged me for avoiding masculine pronouns when referring to God. Chelsey chided me more than once, reminding me that Jesus was a man and the Bible calls God "Father." When Chelsey found an instance of "he" for God in the manuscript, she gave a victorious cheer. As I listen to sermons of younger women from whom I genuinely receive the gospel, I find that Chelsey is right. Once they are away from the seminary where I teach, these preachers also refer to God as "he." As I say good-bye to one collaborator, God graces me with a new source of wisdom and inspiration. I recall Connie telling me that, in the years to come, Chelsey's would be *the* most important voice for me to listen to. Thanks, Connie—and Chelsey!

I am sad Connie was not here to review, correct, and improve the pages that follow. I suspect she would be pleased overall, if only because, where I once approached the stewardship sermon with fear and trepidation, I am now eager for opportunities to preach it. I pray the same thing happens for you as you read this book and discuss it with other leaders in your congregation.

Thank you, Connie, for instilling your love of stewardship in me. With abiding friendship, I dedicate this book to you.

CHAPTER I

What Do We Mean by *Stewardship?*

"SO, YOU'RE WRITING A BOOK about preaching and stewardship?" I am asked. "Yes," I reply, and the questioner continues, "Of course, you're going to include a chapter on . . ." Then I hear about the person's passion, priority, or project framed as some aspect of stewardship—climate change as stewardship of creation, diet and exercise as stewardship of the body, relationship and parenting skills as stewardship of the family, citizenship as stewardship of the common good, vocation as stewardship of the abilities we possess and the responsibilities entrusted to us. The list goes on. Every topic has a prescription—decrease one's carbon footprint, walk thirty minutes a day and cut down on red meat, make a date night with your spouse and spend quality time with your kids, allow your faith to inform your politics, cultivate a spirit of service over self-interest. When I respond that this book is limited to money, the questioner responds disappointedly, "Oh, I thought the book was about stewardship."

"So, you're writing a book about preaching and stewardship?" a second person asks, and when I say that I am, the response is, "That's exactly what we need!" Then the questioner recounts how, every year at the September church council meeting, the treasurer's report indicates that the congregation's budget is running deep in the red. After someone on the board attempts to console the alarmed council by assuring them that people have been away during the summer and that the "big months" still lie ahead, someone else urgently wants to know what the council and congregation are going to do about stewardship. Talk around the council table quickly turns to the stewardship sermon as all eyes turn to the pastor, who gets the distinct and sinking feeling that she or he is supposed to say something in ten or fifteen or twenty minutes on Stewardship Sunday that will make the congregation's deficit woes, if not the deficit itself, disappear.

I confess that at one time I assumed that the meaning of *preaching stewardship* was obvious. I thought that, one way or another, stewardship, at least from a Christian perspective, means giving money—or time, talent, and treasure—to the church. I thought that to *preach* stewardship was to invite people to give in response to God or the gospel. The conversations I had about this book reveal that, in practice, my assumptions about preaching stewardship are false in at least two ways. First, although I am usually talking with Christian pastors or congregational leaders, they understand stewardship as something people do and often make no mention of God or the gospel. The people I am talking with are so sincerely and urgently focused on the issue or concern they understand to be stewardship and what we need to do about it that they presume, overlook, or neglect to mention God. Listening to a lot of preaching tells me that this same thing frequently happens in stewardship sermons.

Second, these conversations reveal that, both in the church and in the culture, *stewardship* is such a code word that many people listening to sermons may not know what preachers are talking about when they preach stewardship. In fact, even preachers and congregational leaders have different ideas of what it means to preach stewardship. Stewardship, as one New Testament scholar observes, "need mean nothing more than fund-raising pure and simple. Or it can extend itself into an all-encompassing, even pretentious, expression that overarches all Christian life and faith."[1] For Douglas John Hall, professor of systematic theology at McGill University in Montreal, stewardship means care of the globe in cooperation with all right-minded, ecologically inclined people, through correct political action for the future of society.[2]

So, the conversations about this book reveal that as preachers and congregational leaders, we are unclear about both what we mean by stewardship and how that relates to God and the gospel. Following the lead of these conversations, I define what I mean by stewardship in this chapter. Then, in chapter 2, I turn to preaching and consider how whatever the preacher and congregational leaders determine to be stewardship relates to God and the gospel.

"If You Mean Money, Say Money!"

To preach stewardship that stands any chance of connecting with people's lives and getting them to respond, preachers and congregational leaders need to define what they mean by *stewardship*. In reality, even when the stewardship sermon is based on appointed Scripture readings, it is a topical sermon. Ronald Allen, who teaches preaching and New Testament at Christian Theological Seminary in Indianapolis, writes, "The topical sermon interprets a topic in light of the gospel but without originating or centering in the exposition of a biblical text or theme."[3] At its best, the topical sermon teaches the congregation how to interpret life in light of the gospel. It models for the congregation how to name or identify an issue, reflect upon it theologically, and claim changes in perception and behavior as a result of that analysis. To accomplish this, preachers cannot assume that stewardship has an inherent meaning that is widely understood. Instead, preachers need to decide what topic they mean by stewardship using a single word—or as few words as possible. Then preachers stop using the word *stewardship* in preaching and use that word or words instead.

As I said, the meaning of stewardship was initially obvious to me. I thought that stewardship meant giving money—or time, talent, and treasure—to the church in response to God or the gospel. In the course of writing this book, I learned that determining what stewardship means for a given faith community at a particular time in its life truly is a matter of discussion, discernment, and decision. For example, some preachers and leaders, and certainly some churchgoers, understand stewardship as church-speak for the congregation's annual fund-raising event. This "necessary evil," as one parishioner called it, is usually held in October or November and includes a once-a-year sermon. In this annual sermon, the preacher makes the case that congregation members increase their giving of money to the church, not in response to God or the gospel but in response to a budget or deficit, or priorities and programming proposed by the church board or congregational council. For other preachers and church leaders, the notion of stewardship has

expanded from the money people promise to put in the offering plate
to embrace everything from how we speak of Jesus and our faith, al-
locate our time, use our talents, take care of our bodies, manage our
finances, and care for creation. Outside the church, stewardship means
many things, including (1) the responsibility for taking care of passen-
gers' domestic needs on a cruise ship or train, (2) managing the service
provided to diners in an exclusive restaurant, (3) a responsibility to take
care of something owned by someone else, (4) an ethic that embodies cooperative planning and management of environmental resources
to prevent loss of habitat and facilitate its recovery in the interest of
long-term sustainability, and (5) a leadership philosophy of service over
self-interest.

In *Stewardship and the Economy of God*, New Testament scholar John
Reumann demonstrates how understanding stewardship in a host of
different ways is nothing new. Professor Reumann studies the Greek
word *oikonomia*, which he translates as "the economy of God" and from
which the concept of stewardship evolved, and related words from historical, linguistic, and theological perspectives. Reumann demonstrates
that, in the course of the church's life, the Christian use of *oikonomia*,
or stewardship, had a wide variety of meanings and applications.[4] For
example, in the patristic period, the word *oikonomia*, whose basic
meaning is the art and science of household management, is used (1)
by Origen and Eusebius for Jesus's incarnation, ministry, passion, and
resurrection; (2) by Irenaeus for redemptive history or God's covenantal
relationships with humanity, Israel, and the church; (3) by Clement of
Alexandria for ethical applications; and (4) by Tertullian to speak of the
Trinity. Reumann suggests each church group and period of history
must provide its own working definition of stewardship and that "no
one image or definition can overarch all aspects of the *oikonomia* theme
without diminishing the breadth and variety of the whole."[5]

Determining a working definition of stewardship invites preachers
and congregational leaders into conversation about the faith community's identity, needs, priorities, and sense of mission. The congregation
whose budget is running deep in the red will arrive at a working definition of stewardship that is different from one chosen by the congregation whose members are quick to pull out their checkbooks but slow
to give their time. A congregation with an outreach ministry to adults
who are homeless will define stewardship differently from a congregation whose outreach ministry is the monthly performance of Bach can-

tatas. The viability of our congregations and of the church also affects how we define stewardship. Many congregations, institutions, and denominations are declining, even dying, because of decreasing support, while others are growing economically and numerically. For those parts of the church in decline, making ends meet is a widespread anxiety and has even become the tacit mission of the church.

Our working definition of stewardship will be shaped by the fact that the church is in a time of profound change. Phyllis Tickle, founding editor of the Religion Department of *Publishers Weekly*, observes, "About every five hundred years the Church feels compelled to hold a giant rummage sale."[6] About every five hundred years, the empowered structures of institutionalized Christianity, whatever those structures happen to be at that time, become an intolerable, self-protecting shell that needs to be shattered so renewal and growth can occur. So the church rummages around its attic and decides what to hang on to and what it needs to let go of. History shows us that, when this happens, (1) a new, more vital form of Christianity emerges; (2) the dominant organizational expression of Christianity is reconstituted into a purer and less ossified expression of its former self; (3) in the process of gaining a brand new expression of its faith and practice, the church also gains a grand refurbishment of its older one; and (4) every time established Christianity is broken open, that faith has spread—and been spread—dramatically into new geographic and demographic areas. In other words, the unease and distress of the rummage sale gives way to a broader and deeper Christian faith. So, for example, five hundred years ago, the Protestant Reformation both established a new, powerful way of being Christian and forced Roman Catholicism to make changes in its own structures and practice, with the result that Christianity spread over more of the earth than it had in the past. Five hundred years before that, the church experienced the Great Schism. We are living through one of those five-hundred-year rummage sales today.

The history of the Protestant church in the United States indicates that factors beyond the congregation, including the state of the economy, the health of a denomination, and how a congregation views the greater church, and even people's understanding of their nation's place in the world affect how a congregation defines stewardship. For instance, asking people to give their time is difficult when they are working three jobs to make ends meet. It also is easier to support the denomination when a congregation agrees with the denomination's stand on social issues. Christians in the United States were more eager to support "world missions" during periods in history like World War II, when they regarded the United States as "a light to the nations" (Isa. 42:6; 49:6).

As I write this book, congregations' working definitions of stewardship are shaped by a recession, which we are told is over even as people cannot find employment and pay their bills, particularly their mortgages. An understanding of stewardship is also shaped by the truth that in American culture, religion is a consumer-driven enterprise in which individuals obtain resources appropriate to the faith, spirituality, or relationship with God they seek from many highly differentiated outlets, ranging from traditional churches to the religion, spirituality, healing, and self-help sections of bookstores to Oprah. Like so many other commodities, people can have whatever kind of religion they are willing to pay for—and a considerable amount of religion for free.

Determining a working definition of stewardship can be difficult and time consuming. Depending on its situation, a congregation might change the definition from year to year or even sermon to sermon. Moreover, not providing a working definition and assuming everyone knows what we are talking about often makes preaching easier and more comfortable for the one in the pulpit and some who listen to the sermon. The preacher can dance around how people use their money, time, and skills and avoid asking the congregation to respond by talking about stewardship as an all-encompassing umbrella and never getting specific. Yet, this approach to preaching stewardship frequently fails to connect with those sitting in the pews, because they are not sure what the preacher is talking about. Listeners can keep things vague, theoretical, and even pious and never allow the sermon to find its way into their calendars, checkbooks, and to-do lists. For preaching stewardship to matter, preachers need to name what they mean by stewardship. As one congregant told his pastor, "If you mean money, say money."

For the purposes of this book, I confine my working definition of *stewardship* to what Professor Reumann implies is the "crass" association of the word with money and fund-raising for the church. Professor Reumann suggests that at its most basic—or perhaps its most base—definition, stewardship is concerned with "the necessary matter of meeting (and possibly exceeding) budgets and devising equitable ways for all congregations of a denomination to share in a total budget."[7] I recognize others would have me include chapters on their passions and priorities. I would surely find it edifying to take a more expansive or panoramic view of stewardship. Yet, I am keenly aware that the annual stewardship sermon or sermons is a reality that every preacher faces, often with a certain level of anxiety, if not outright fear and trepidation. This preaching event is my focus. My definition of stewardship is what I have always understood stewardship to be—giving money to the church in response to the gospel. Yet, while my concern in this book is with money and giving, I suspect the observations I offer are applicable to other stewardship topics that preachers and congregations may wish to address through preaching. Therefore, some readers might choose to approach this book as a case study.

More important than how I define stewardship and my rationale for defining stewardship solely in terms of money, my first point about preaching stewardship is that preachers and congregational leaders need to define stewardship for themselves and for their hearers. Once a congregation's leaders agree on a working definition, preachers define stewardship for their hearers and preach sermons that better connect with them by minimizing or eliminating their use of this churchy code word and saying plainly what they are talking about—money, volunteering, diet and exercise, care of creation, ministry in daily life, whatever. "If you mean money, say money."

Stewardship and Money

Once preachers and congregational leaders define stewardship, preachers should learn all they can about the topic. Ronald Allen suggests that the preacher's learning most surely includes the origin and history of the topic, its current manifestation and all the issues related to it, and theological resources with which to understand and evaluate it.[8] My study of money and giving to the church, particularly its history in North America, reveals six characteristics of the stewardship of money and giving to the church that shape preaching stewardship in important ways. First, the church invented stewardship. Second, stewardship is more pragmatic than theological; it is a practice born of necessity and in search of a theology. Third, at some level, ministers are anxious about preaching about money and giving because of the tension between needing to raise their own salaries and their sincere belief that God and humanity are served through giving to the church. Fourth, stewardship as a discipline was introduced in response to appeals from competing causes as a way of securing a larger portion of what people gave for the local church. Fifth, churchgoers have learned well that the church building is the most worthwhile cause of all. Sixth, preaching about money and giving has been tethered with Christian formation and fund-raising techniques.

Invented by the Church

Many preachers and congregational leaders assume that ways of practicing stewardship—including spoken and unspoken norms about how the preacher will (or will not) address money from the pulpit, the form or format of the annual stewardship campaign and budgeting process, and ways of receiving congregants' responses—are something "we've always done this way." Preachers and leaders may even assume "the way we've always done it" is the way God wants stewardship done, as if stories of giving in the Bible—Abraham giving Melchizedek a tenth (Gen. 14:20), Israel bringing "first fruits" into the house of the Lord (Exod. 23:19; 34:22), the people putting their gifts into the temple treasury as Jesus looked on (Mark 12:41; Luke 21:1), the church after Pentecost distributing the proceeds from the sale of their possessions to all according to their needs (Acts 2:44–45), and Paul's collection for the church at Jerusalem (1 Cor. 16:1–3)—are instances of an unchanging stewardship practice that extends throughout the biblical narrative and church's life to our day as ushers pass plates, bags, or baskets each Sunday in worship. Many preachers and leaders therefore approach the way they always ask for and give money to the church as an unchanging feature of congregational life instituted or commanded by God.

To effectively preach about money and giving, preachers give up the notion that God instituted the way they have *always* done stewardship and recognize that, like worship practices and biblical interpretation, stewardship is a way the church attempts to faithfully respond to God and the gospel, and this faithful response has changed over time. Throughout this book, I repeatedly assert that God is unquestionably concerned about what people do with and how we relate to money. For example, God prohibits Israel from lending money to the poor at interest (Exod. 22:25; Lev. 25:37) and commands a census tax to provide money for the services of the tent of meeting (Exod. 30:12–16). Through the prophet Amos, God condemns exploiting the poor for money and love of money that leads to cheating (Amos 2:6; 8:4–8). As

I explore in chapter 2, Jesus has lots to say about money. Yet, God does not give us a single, eternal, divinely authorized practice of giving money to the church.

For many Christians, the church *always* appealed to the faithful for voluntary giving. Yet, the church has used many other approaches to raise money. I just noted that in Exodus, God commands a census tax to pay for the services of the tent of meeting. For centuries, cathedrals and parish churches were built using gifts from the nobility, and benefactors provided for the clergy. The church sold indulgences and collected taxes. Today, congregations hold harvest dinners and spaghetti suppers and publish and sell cookbooks. In his study of the economic history of North American Protestantism over the course of the past 250 years, *In Pursuit of the Almighty's Dollar: A History of Money*, James Hudnut-Beumler, who teaches church history at Vanderbilt Divinity School, demonstrates that as a church practice related to money and voluntary giving, stewardship is a peculiarly North American phenomena. At different times during its life in America, the church has understood giving money for the church in many different ways and has engaged in diverse practices and approaches that followed from its understanding. In the process, stewardship as voluntary giving to the church has searched for rather than grown from the church's theology and has had a checkered history of vitality in some periods and apathy in others.[9] Those who study stewardship see this diversity in theological perspective and response in contemporary approaches to preaching about money, which range from giving out of gratitude for blessings received to giving to receive blessings to giving so as not to anger God by violating a divine command.

Since the church does not have a single, eternal, divinely authorized approach to stewardship, preachers must determine what for them is a faithful approach to preaching about money and giving. A preacher's and faith community's theology of stewardship is shaped by factors including how they understand the gospel, the Bible, the preaching task, and the nature of the church. For example, preachers and faith communities might approach giving money to the church as a biblical law or obligation, a faith or discipleship practice, or, as the title of this book suggests, as God's invitation to grow. Each approach reflects a different theological perspective. I will offer my perspective and say more about preaching in response to the gospel in chapter 2. Here, I simply make the point that the way one preaches stewardship must be consistent with the preacher's and faith community's theological perspective. At the same time, the way one preaches stewardship must also produce results. In fact, history indicates that the need to produce results has often caused the church's approaches to stewardship to be more pragmatic than theological.

More Pragmatic than Theological

The approaches to money and giving that came to be known as stewardship were invented in the United States during the years from approximately 1885 to the end of World War I, as church leaders joined the culture in celebrating the multiplying and transforming power of money. Advocates of stewardship asserted that, through gifts of money, the faithful Christian participates in the church's mission and ministry in many ways and many places simultaneously, both at home and around the world, thereby multiplying the work of the kingdom of God. For example, Professor Hudnut-Beumler reports that, in a book entitled *Our Christian Stewardship* (1910), John Wesley Duncan observed, "Money was like electricity; it was stored power, and the question was whether the battery in which it was stored would do wonders, such as curing a severe pain, or cause death in an electric chair."[10]

To harness the power of money for the work of God's kingdom, advocates of stewardship argued against tithing, the prevailing approach to raising money for the church, which was proving less effective than it had once been. They declared that Christians did not need a divine command or obligation to give a share of their own property to God. Rather, Christians needed to understand themselves as trustees or managers or stewards of God's property. God did not have a right to a tithe or one-tenth of an individual's possessions; God had a right to ten-tenths, because God owns everything. Since everything belongs to God, Christians are to use everything they possess in a way that will best honor God and serve the work of God's kingdom. Rather than discharging one's obligation by consecrating a tenth to the Lord, stewardship is a form of discipleship. Using everything they possess to honor God and serve God's kingdom is a way Christians deny themselves, take up a cross, and follow Jesus.

The birth of stewardship illustrates that the ways the church understood and approached giving money to the church were overwhelmingly pragmatic; they resulted from the need to raise money more than from theological convictions and biblical perspectives. In this instance, the advocates of stewardship found a theology that corresponded favorably to the positive appraisal of money's power prevalent in the culture at the time and addressed tithing's waning success. This is not an isolated instance. Throughout the church's history in the United States, stewardship's pragmatic character is evident in the fact that Protestants across traditions preach about money in the same ways. While evangelicals, fundamentalists, dispensationalists, Pentecostals, and mainline Protestants are divided by their beliefs, worship practices, patterns of church leadership, and stands on social issues, Protestants are united in their practices of raising money for the church based on a few biblical precedents and in response to cultural patterns.

Professor Hudnut-Beumler shows that the greatest changes in giving money to and raising money for the church resulted from what he calls the "great privatization," that is, "the relocation of religion from a public good to a private, voluntarily supported good."[11] In Colonial America, asking people to give money to the church was unnecessary because supporting the only church in the colony was part of belonging to the community. Since the church building was the largest, and usually only, public assembly space in a town, it was where taxes were set to support the public's business, including providing for the worship of God. In one way or another, community funds were used to build the church, and rates (or taxes), including renting pews to families according to their rank in the community, provided the funds for the minister, who by virtue of his education, served as a public official as well as a spiritual leader.

Everything changed between 1750 and 1800 as American society redefined who was obliged to support a minister and church. Starting with the Great Awakening of the 1730s and 1740s, people were freed to follow and support ministers of their own choosing. People tended to support ministers whom they determined possessed an authentic faith and calling and not merely an education and a contract with a town to preach. Even those who remained loyal to long-term ministers and parishes began to do so with the awareness that they were making a choice rather than fulfilling an obligation. The Bill of Rights (1791) ratified that there was no one church for all states and peoples. Freedom of religion meant that ministers lost their status as public officials, and by 1800 the church lost its public financing. Hudnut-Beumler explains, "As the Revolution began, ten of the original thirteen states had some form of tax-supported religion. In 1833, with the final elimination of commonwealth support for the Congregational Church in Massachusetts, every religious group was left to its own resources."[12] Religious freedom and privatization directly challenged the notion that the public should pay for the church because religion is a public good.

Rather than responding out of an established theological perspective, church leaders reasoned that because the churches were good for the public, any means the public accepted for raising the money necessary for their perpetuation was as good as any other means. Therefore, churches initially continued to receive money from poll and property taxes, which could be quite high. Yet, as congregations moved from the public sphere into the private sector, churches had available only two broad models for support: the private club and the voluntary member-supported institution.[13] In a private club, people cannot take advantage of the benefits of the club and its services without paying the assessed dues or apportionments, and the organization sets the price. If you want to belong to the club, you pay the dues. So, for example, Professor Hudnut-Beumler compares a congregation to a country club and reports, "Religious groups charged pew rents and ostracized those who used the 'free' pews in the back of the church."[14] The church understandably had two problems with this approach, one theological and the other practical. Theologically, people did not have to pay for a relationship with God, and the church ought not allow money in the form of membership dues to stand between people and God. Practically, the presence of more than one Protestant church in most communities by midway through the nineteenth century meant that people could go elsewhere for a relationship with God. Still, someone had to pay for the church and its ministers. So congregations, recognizing that they were dependent upon the voluntary contributions of their members, offered themselves as privately supported public goods, in the same way that public radio does today. Thus, what the church today knows as stewardship was born of necessity.

Stewardship preaching is *practical theology* in the truest sense of the term. Its spiritual aim is to help people deepen their faith and grow in grace by giving in response to the gospel. At the same time, preachers are expected to produce the financial resources their congregations need. The *practical* and *theological* aims of stewardship preaching are regularly at odds with each other. Stewardship preaching that invites people to deepen their faith and grow in grace works slowly, in small but significant ways, and changes people and faith communities over weeks, years, and lifetimes. In other words, preaching that invites people to grow in giving in response to the gospel tends to be impractical. It does not speak directly to the material needs of the church and, therefore, does not produce the profound or immediate monetary results that many preachers and leaders desire and many congregations need. Preaching about money and giving therefore reveals an inherent tension between preaching to shape people's values, attitudes, habits, and behavior over time and preaching to produce the financial resources the church needs today. I say more about the results of preaching stewardship in chapter 7. Here, my third point about preaching stewardship is that, by understanding what preaching can and cannot accomplish, preachers recognize that, because financial needs are more immediate and tangible, the tension, even temptation, is to do what works and preach in ways that are more pragmatic than theological. By being aware of this tension, preachers are better able to determine how to balance theological integrity and practical necessity. Preachers and congregational leaders can also better negotiate the minefield of yielding to and resisting the temptation to do whatever works to raise the money the congregation needs.

Anxiety for the Preacher

If you are suddenly feeling anxious or uncomfortable, you are not alone. Historically, the tension between giving money in response to the gospel and the church's need for money created anxiety for the preacher as the privatization of religion in American society turned "every pastor, however willing or able, into a development officer among his own people."[15] As a result, preachers became uncomfortable preaching to raise money, because they knew a large portion of that money would pay their salaries. On the one hand, they resented the need to raise their own support. On the other hand, preachers genuinely believed that people serve God through giving as the church serves humanity.

As many preachers know firsthand, the anxiety caused by the tension between the material realities of church life and the spiritual practice of giving in response and service to God persists to our day.

To address this tension and promote giving, preachers downplayed the material realities of religious life. Instead of talking about the financial support the churches (and their ministers) needed, preachers developed an ever-changing but persistent rhetoric that intensely spiritualized giving. They repeatedly invoked God, ecclesiastical tradition, and scriptural evidence, to a greater degree than did the European churches from which most of the US churches were descended. Particularly during the years between the Revolution and the Civil War, the ways that religious groups raised money became more and more steeped in religious rationale, biblical precedent, and the language of sacred obligation as preachers concluded that the Bible had something to say about how Christians ought to give. Yet, it was not until the period from 1870 to 1920 that church leaders undertook to deduce the biblically correct mode of supporting the church by reading the Bible more correctly than any readers had done before and to create the right system for raising and collecting support. Along the way, nearly every church leader would come to adopt the word *stewardship* to describe his or her aims and practice. I discuss the Bible and stewardship in chapter 3.

Each generation of preachers sought to negotiate the tension between the material and spiritual aspects of asking for money and to raise the resources necessary to support the churches' ministries in ways appropriate to the ecclesial and societal realties of its day. Yet, in every generation, most religious accounts of why people should support their churches posit a relationship between human beings and God, who is beyond the human community. We are taught that the only way to give money to God is to give it to a mediating human institution, such as a church, or perhaps to engage in direct charity on behalf of God by providing for someone as God might do if God were here. Thus religious people give to God by giving to the religious institutions they support and by giving directly to someone in need.[16]

For their part, parishioners both cooperated with and resisted their ministers—by giving and withholding their money, and by participating in and staying away from church. During periods when the economy was good, faith was assumed, and the church was revered, people gave enough money to support God and the church that individual congregations and denominations secured their own future and guaranteed that competing religious entities had exactly the same opportunities and resources. In addition to funding congregations and supporting their ministers, Christians financed voluntary societies and helped enlarge what the Protestant church considered its mission, whose expanded scope and structure then drove the need for yet more money.

Today, financial considerations force many congregations, church institutions, and denominations to determine what is essential to their ministries and to let go of everything that is not, and even to contemplate the possibility of their demise. The need for financial resources has introduced increasing competition, even within denominations, as religious entities vie for a greater share of a shrinking pool of resources. The situation is further complicated by the fact that the increasing costs of operating a congregation, particularly ministerial support, coupled with the loss of a focus on mission and service to the world, lead many Christians to acknowledge that God's work in the world is not confined to the church, rendering the historic understanding of the relationship between God and humanity—give to God by giving to the church—less credible. This change in understanding may explain why stewardship sermons emphasize giving in response to a need rather than explicitly in response to God. These are anxious times, and preachers should expect a certain level of anxiety about preaching about money and giving. Yet, preachers can manage their anxiety by uncovering assumptions—their own and their hearers'—about money and giving, and preaching about these things. This is the topic of chapter 7.

Competitor with Worthy Causes

Preachers and congregational leaders frequently complain that people are eager to give to particular causes but hesitant to give to the ongoing work of the church. This is nothing new. In fact, once church leaders realized they were dependent upon people's voluntary giving, appealing to worthy causes was among the first means they used to obtain the money necessary to maintain the church's mission beyond paying a congregation's bills. In the United States, the church has a rich history of inviting church members to contribute to worthwhile causes beyond their own congregations. From the early nineteenth century through today, representatives of causes—including training pastors, supporting missionaries, providing for denominational institutions and ministries, and caring for the poor, sick, and forgotten—have crisscrossed the country asking pastors for time in their congregations' worship to make a case for supporting the particular cause and to ask for funds. The more compelling the testimony is—describing the need for disaster relief, for example, as opposed to the need to refurbish the bishop's office—the better are the results. Local church finance seems tame and boring compared to special causes, so at times the church has looked upon these causes as direct competitors for the support people give their congregations.

In response to this competition, church leaders decided to encourage voluntary giving in a systematic manner, which they could better control, by appealing for unified giving in the church. They argued that church people, overwhelmed by the claims of worthwhile causes on their tithes and offerings, desire more information to help them determine how to disburse their gifts, but in the end either do nothing or give only to what seems to them to be the most urgent cause. Rather than inviting people to give in response to individual causes, the church taught that people were to cultivate a habit by giving a portion of their income to the church for charitable uses. Some church leaders appealed to the distribution principle modeled in Acts, by which goods were held in common after Pentecost and distributed "as any had need" (2:45). Others cited 1 Corinthians 16:1–2: "Now concerning the collection for the saints: you should follow the directions I gave to the churches of Galatia. On the first day of every week, each of you is to put aside and save whatever extra you earn, so that collections need not be taken when I come." Here they found a discipline or rule, binding on all the faithful, that a portion of their income be set apart and given to the church on the Sabbath for charitable causes. People were to support the church's mission through giving to their congregation. Nevertheless, giving to causes remains prevalent in the church. This is nowhere more evident than in the money given to construct, improve, and maintain church buildings.

Anything for the Building

Pastors and congregational leaders frequently complain people will give any amount of money for the church building at the same time as they attempt to save money by cutting spending on the congregation's mission and ministry. In a sense, this is an instance of people learning well what the church taught them. In the years leading up to the Civil War, US Protestants established the lasting pattern of building churches as needed, and rebuilding and improving churches as acts of devotion and self-expression. Hudnut-Beumler notes, "Each generation of pastors and people made the church building its own, bringing the fashions of the day from their homes into the house of God. All the while, they closely watched what other churches were building in terms of style and features. Mimicking one another, Protestant congregations assured themselves that no one church would pull too far ahead when it came to being attractive and offering the finest work of human hands to God."[17]

Church buildings are tangible expressions of the faith and devotion of people personally and directly involved in worshiping God at a particular time and in a particular place. A church building proclaims how a faith community conceives of and experiences God, relates to its neighbors, and understands the church's mission or the purpose that God expects the church to serve. Church buildings are one way congregations draw the people they want to attract and show how they are different from (and superior to) other congregations. Moreover, by building a beautiful church, people can indulge their taste for beauty and even a modicum of luxury without committing the sin of personal indulgence or ostentation, because the church is God's house and therefore worthy of any luxury or expense.

In the process of building and rebuilding churches, US Protestants established a long-term pattern of nearly constant investment in bricks and mortar. The church's investment in church buildings is so great that housing congregations has consumed more of church finances than any other activity except compensating the clergy, and has provided a regular incentive to give more money. The emphasis on building and the amount of money congregations raise for and invest in church buildings are so great that buildings have shaped the prevailing American conception of the church. In the United States, *church* is a building; church is the place where one goes to church, or the place where others go to church. Only secondarily is the church a body of people that gathers for worship and fellowship. Despite theologians' and ministers' best efforts, the word *church* rarely means something beyond the local congregation, such as the denomination or "holy catholic and apostolic church." Giving to the church seems to correspond with this understanding. Assuming people are on good terms with their congregations, they tend to give first to the building, then to their local faith community, and finally to the church beyond the congregation. Responding to this trend, church leaders have tethered preaching with fund-raising techniques to raise the money they need.

Tethered with Technique

By 1920, despite growing domestic prosperity, missionary agencies at home and abroad began to notice significant decline in receipts. Different techniques for raising money and different ways of thinking about giving for church causes began to be employed more freely. By the end of World War II, the church had partnered preaching stewardship concepts with fund-raising techniques. The three most pronounced and lasting fund-raising techniques used are (1) the every-member canvass or visitation, (2) pledge cards, and (3) the divided envelope, on which church members specify what portion of their weekly offering is to be given to the congregation and what portion given to benevolence. Christians are trained to give to the church at a very young age as children are taught the importance of giving in Sunday school. Over the years, the fund-raising techniques employed by the church have expanded to encompass direct mail appeals, encouraging people to include giving to the church in the family budget, using church budgets to articulate needs before asking for money, marketing, advertising, fund-raising events, a fee-for-service approach to church life, and paying with a credit card and through automatic withdrawal from bank accounts.

For good and for ill, the stewardship sermon is not a solo act. For preaching to be effective, preachers and congregational leaders must plan so that preaching and the congregation's stewardship or fund-raising campaign complement rather than contradict each other. Ideally, preaching *anchors* whatever fund-raising techniques the congregation uses in the gospel and holds them accountable to the gospel that is preached. At the same time, the congregation's fund-raising techniques either *amplify* or *undermine* preaching.[18] When preaching and fund-raising techniques are congruent, the message of the sermon is amplified. The place of preaching is enhanced, because the congregation experiences preaching the gospel as something that leadership takes seriously. On the other hand, when preaching and the congregation's fund-raising techniques are not congruent, people trust their own experience more than the preacher's words. The power of preaching is diminished, because the sermon's message is undermined or even contradicted by what the congregation is doing to secure the money it needs.

Perhaps a congregation's best way of negotiating the relationship between preaching and fund-raising techniques is for pastors and other leaders to openly discuss how much the church is and is not like a business or charity. In the way it raises and spends money, what does it mean for the church to be in the world but not of the world (John 17:13–16)? I discuss the partnership of preaching and other aspects of congregational stewardship further in chapter 8.

In this chapter, I have attempted to demonstrate the importance of explicitly defining stewardship in preaching, and I discussed six characteristics of giving to the church that shape how preachers preach. Any of these attributes—the theology we choose, pragmatism, anxiety, emphasizing causes, understanding the church primarily as building, and the use of fund-raising techniques—can challenge and even overwhelm God's invitation to grow in response to the gospel of Jesus Christ. This is evident in sermons in which preachers are so sincerely and urgently focused on money and giving that they presume, overlook, or neglect to mention God. So, in chapter 2, I assert that to *preach* stewardship is to proclaim the unconditional love of God revealed in Jesus Christ and only then to invite people to grow in giving in response to the gospel. Otherwise, preachers are simply fund-raising from the pulpit by talking about the need to give money to the church.

AS YOU PREPARE YOUR SERMON . . .

- What single word do you mean by stewardship?
- What does your and your congregation's way of asking for money for the church say about who God is?
- How long has your congregation done stewardship the same way? What about the way you do stewardship might be helpful to change? What are the risks of changing?
- In dealing with money, in what ways is the church like and not like a business? Like and not like a charity?

CHAPTER 2

Why Should We Grow in Giving?

"WHY SHOULD I GIVE to the church?" Or, "Why should I grow in my giving to the church?" Bottom line: stewardship sermons need to answer this question. Since my concern in this book is money, the question becomes more precise: "Why should I give money to the church or grow in my giving of money to the church?" Whether preachers and congregational leaders define stewardship as money or something else, we need to answer the question, why should people give to the church? We have at our disposal lots of ways of answering it. Yet, when we answer this question from the pulpit, the answer we give says something about who we proclaim God is, whether we realize it or not.

"Why should I give to the church?" If we tell people to give in order to get, people might conclude that God is like a crooked politician whose favor we can purchase. That's what Simon the magician thought in Acts. "Now when Simon saw that the Spirit was given through the laying on of the apostles' hands, he offered them money, saying, 'Give me also this power so that anyone on whom I lay my hands may receive the Holy Spirit'" (Acts 8:18–19). If we tell people to give out of obedience to a divine command to tithe, God might become an angry judge who demands and enforces. We can find plenty of verses like this one that tell us to fear the Lord. "Set apart a tithe of all the yield of your seed that is brought in yearly from the field . . . so that you may learn to fear the LORD your God always" (Deut. 14:22–23). If we tell people to give out of gratitude, people might understand God to be the source of everything we are and all we have, and that God lovingly provides for us. We might truly take what Jesus said to heart: "Do not worry about your life, what you will eat or what you will drink, or about your body, what you will wear. . . . Look at the birds of the air. . . . Are you not of more value than they? . . . Consider the lilies of the field . . . will [God] not much more clothe you—you of little faith? Therefore do not worry, saying, 'What will we eat?' or 'What will we drink?' or 'What will we wear?'" (Matt. 6:25–31).

"Why should I give to the church?" When preachers answer this question, the answers we give are limited, because we need to be especially careful to answer in a way that is consistent with who we proclaim God to be. Otherwise, we offer an inconsistent or contradictory message. We cannot, for example, preach that God loves people unconditionally and saves them by grace and then imply that they somehow earn God's love and favor by how much they give—even if this approach is more effective in garnering the money the church needs. When people experience inconsistency or a contradictory message in preaching, they tend to resonate more with what they are told they need to do than with who the preacher says God is. More than misleading listeners, such a sermon undermines the gospel.

Whether the topic is money and giving or anything else, preachers cannot forget the primary purpose of the sermon. From a Christian perspective, to *preach* is first and foremost to proclaim the good news "that God's love, confirmed in Jesus Christ, is freely, graciously, offered to each and all, and . . . that we are to love God with our whole selves and to love and do justice to our neighbors as ourselves."[1] To preach stewardship, then, is to proclaim the gospel in such a way that Christians respond by giving their money, spending their time, using their abilities, or however we define stewardship in response and service to Christ, often by supporting Christ's church—specifically, the congregation. Somehow, preaching stewardship is a response to God or the gospel. In this regard, the stewardship sermon is different from the fund-raising appeal made by the symphony, an alma mater, or the cancer society.

The point of this chapter, and my fourth point about preaching money and giving, is that people use their money and give to the church in response to the gospel. In this chapter I explore some of the possibilities, limitations, and implications for preaching about money and giving that flow from proclaiming the gospel. These include (1) preaching is not fund-raising; (2) God, not money, is the subject of the sermon; (3) preachers must name the *good news* in giving; (4) exhortation follows proclamation; (5) Jesus does the talking; (6) the gospel calls for invitation; and (7) the sermon appeals to the best in people, to their identity as God's beloved children.

I was once privileged to serve as the "opening act" for Martin E. Marty, one of the most prominent interpreters of religion and culture today. When Dr. Marty took the stage, he described me as a "one trick pony." "All you hear from Satterlee," Marty declared, "is 'Preach the gospel! Preach the gospel! Preach the gospel!'" Those familiar with my work will find that, as usual, Marty is correct. This chapter includes themes that I regularly teach in my classes, advocate when speaking at conferences, and have written about elsewhere. When it comes to preaching the gospel, I am a one trick pony. "Thankfully," Marty concluded, "a reminder to preach the gospel is what most preachers need to hear." The other reminder about the annual stewardship sermon I need to hear as a preacher is that preaching about money or stewardship is not fund-raising from the pulpit.

Preaching Is Not Fund-raising from the Pulpit

I am genuinely impressed at the way public radio stations unabashedly ask for the money they need. They highlight public radio's unique mission, excellent quality, and public service. They appeal to listeners' self-interest in terms of both the time that members of the radio audience spend listening to the station and the importance of preserving listeners' favorite programs. Public radio appeals to people's character, both positively and negatively, by hinting that good people pay for the services they use, rather than freeloading from others, and care enough about the things they value to become part of a community committed to preserving those ideals and services. Public radio stations also express their appreciation with rewards, special opportunities, and gifts. They do all this without apology, embarrassment, discomfort, or shame, because they are so convinced of the value of the product and service they provide.

Congregations needing to raise money can and do use these same fund-raising techniques, often to great success. They frame people's giving of money to the church as a response to a given need, the congregation's performance, a budget or budgetary shortfall, or people's attitudes and feelings. The preacher might appeal to a special project, such as a new roof. As I said in chapter 1, the church in the United States has a rich history of inviting people to contribute to worthwhile causes and special projects, and of partnering those invitations with fund-raising techniques. The more the preacher can make the project sound urgent and compelling, the better the results will be. For example, the best time to appeal for a new roof is undoubtedly a rainy Sunday morning when the worship space is cluttered with buckets collecting the raindrops that find their way through the church's leaky roof. The best way to make the appeal might be to divide the cost of the roof by the number of shingles needed to cover it and sell shingles at the resulting price.

The preacher might point to the congregation's mission, to all the good things the church is doing, as if to say, "This is a worthwhile institution" or "This is a good investment." The preacher highlights the benefits the congregation provides members and the positive difference the congregation makes in the community and the world. Closely related, the preacher might appeal to people's sense of gratitude for or loyalty to the congregation, inviting people to *give back* for all the benefits they receive or have received in the past. This is perhaps a better approach when a congregation's mission was more vital in the past, and members appreciate the congregation's legacy and want to preserve it.

Some congregations make the annual budget the impetus for giving and ask people to contribute their *fair share*. Leaders might divide the total budget by the number of giving units to provide a benchmark for giving. In this fee-for-service or member-dues approach, congregational leaders often attempt to demonstrate that they are spending the congregation's money prudently and asking only for what is absolutely necessary. For their part, some congregational members genuinely appreciate this approach, because it employs a business model and does not theologize or spiritualize necessary giving. Some leaders want congregants to understand themselves as members of a club or group who pay the required dues. Interestingly, rather than viewing themselves as club members, some parishioners see themselves as consumers who pay for what they receive apart from committing to the faith or the church. Still other members of the congregation carefully scrutinize and even quibble over the budget, cutting what they deem extravagant or superfluous, as they determine whether the congregation's leadership deserves their continued or increased giving. Sometimes, members of the congregation will move to amend or decrease the budget so that they do not have to increase their giving.

Appealing for money in response to an urgent need, the congregation's performance, people's attitudes and feelings, or the annual budget is not bad or inappropriate. In fact, in critical times, these fund-raising techniques may be a congregation's best way of generating the money it urgently needs. The issue is that these ways of answering the question of why people should give to the church, or grow in their giving, are not *preaching*. While God and the gospel might be implied or assumed, they are not the explicit answer to the question, "Why should I give money to the church or grow in my giving of money to the church?"

"We preach Christ crucified," Paul declares, "a stumbling block to Jews and foolishness to Gentiles, but to those who are the called, both Jews and Greeks, Christ the power of God and the wisdom of God" (1 Cor. 1:23–24, transl. mine). When the need to raise money is urgent, proclaiming Christ crucified can strike us as foolish and, in fact, turn out to be a stumbling block to success. Yet, preaching is the proclamation of the good news of Jesus Christ. As tempting as it is to do what is expedient or popular, to say what is burning in the preacher's heart, to give the correct answer, and to outline the best course of action, preaching is always a word from God about God's love—for us and all creation—and the new life that God brings in Jesus Christ. It is inappropriate and even dishonest to pull a kind of bait and switch and replace what people expect in a sermon—the promise of God's unconditional love, forgiveness, justice, and participation in God's own life revealed in the life, death, and resurrection of Jesus Christ—with a fund-raising appeal. When congregational leadership determines that a fund-raising appeal is necessary, this appeal should never replace the sermon. In fact, making such an appeal from the pulpit is confusing. Some preachers and congregational leaders argue that, when a fund-raising appeal is made in the worship service, it is best that a congregational leader other than the preacher make that appeal to distinguish the proclamation of the gospel from an appeal about the financial needs of the congregation. In these ways, we avoid fund-raising from the pulpit.

God, Not Money, Is the Subject

Because our goal is to preach the gospel, sermons are about God, even as preachers clearly define stewardship so that parishioners know what they mean. I say this for more than theological reasons. Research indicates that people seem at times desperate to hear about God, and people are not hearing all they want to know about God from the pulpit.[2] People want to know who God is, what God is like, and then how God expects us to live or behave. No matter how we define stewardship—as a matter of money and giving, skills and volunteering, time management, health and wholeness, the state of the planet—stewardship is not the explicit subject of the sermon. God is!

I am not saying that all the topics that stewardship encompasses do not belong in the pulpit. As I have written elsewhere, if we follow Jesus's example, every issue is fair game for preaching; no topic is out of bounds. To say otherwise is to identify areas of life where Jesus has no place.[3] Yet, I recall with regret stewardship sermons, ones that I have both preached and heard, so intent on getting the congregation to increase its giving that Jesus was lost somewhere in the background, if he was mentioned at all. The question is not whether but how we address these topics in preaching.

However we define stewardship, the topic or subject must be grounded in and related to the biblical story of God's own work of reconciling, recreating, and righting the world. As both a Christian preacher and a Christian who listens to sermons, I increasingly desire that the stewardship topic be linked to God's will and work as revealed in the life, death, and resurrection of Jesus Christ. We might also speak of God as creator, God's gift of creation, God's ongoing re-creation and renewal of the world, and our participation in this work. Not everyone agrees on how strong and explicit the link between God and the stewardship topic needs to be. Some preachers and congregations demand, and some understandings of stewardship require, that the connection between gospel proclamation and the stewardship topic being addressed be stronger and more explicit than others. As I have written elsewhere, "When people cannot miss the relationship between even the most difficult or controversial issue or sensitive topic and the gospel, when the connection is inescapable, when they are convinced that God has something important to say, preachers and congregants may well feel uncomfortable, but most will listen as God speaks to and through them."[4]

I am not saying that the gospel or biblical narrative is the only reason to give. People regularly and generously give money in response to individual and social needs, their time to causes they value, and their commitment to care for creation in response to the state of the planet. Yet, when it comes to sermons about giving money or anything to the church, we give in response to God or the gospel. Sermons need to provide a declaration—even better, an experience—of God, grace, or the gospel for the congregation to respond to. Then, the movement of the sermon becomes, in the words of Scripture, "We love because [Christ] first loved us" (1 John 4:19).

When God is the subject of the sermon, God is the first and primary actor. In Christ, God does more than call us to give or help us to give. God gives, and then God both invites and empowers us to participate in what God is giving and doing. As Paul writes, "For the love of Christ urges us on" (2 Cor. 5:14). Having listened to hundreds of sermons of all stripes, I am increasingly convinced that preachers fail to make God the subject of the sermon for particular reasons. When preachers make a problem, need, issue, or situation the sermon's theme or topic, relegating God or Christ to an example, helper, or motivator, or leaving God out altogether, it is an indication that the preacher (1) doesn't trust the Holy Spirit to get people to respond and so takes this responsibility upon herself or himself, (2) doesn't believe in the power of the gospel and wants to wield some other power, (3) has an agenda other than preaching, or (4) has not experienced the power of the gospel in preaching and so does not proclaim the gospel large or strong or compelling enough in the sermon. I would even dare say that the more intensely the preacher tries to get the congregation to respond, the more one of these is true.

So, rather than giving a talk on money, rather than outlining a need, preachers do better to preach about God, particularly as God reveals God's very self to us in the life, death, and resurrection of Jesus Christ, and then move to the possibilities and implications of the gospel for our use of money. For example, when preachers make God the subject of the stewardship sermon, the story of the widow's mite (Mark 12:41–44; Luke 21:1–4) is not about the widow or how much she put in the treasury but about God, who is so trustworthy that the widow could "put in everything she had, all she had to live on" (Mark 12:44). When stewardship is grounded in and flows from a clear and bold proclamation of the gospel and does not replace it, and when God is the subject of the sermon, giving is a response to God's grace, because the sermon provides a word from God, or an experience of God, that people can respond to.

Preachers Must Name the Good News in Giving

Giving in response to the gospel does not mean that preachers avoid asking people to give or that they ask timidly or tentatively. In fact, people expect to be asked. "How much should I give?" someone new to the congregation inquired. Embarrassed and a bit befuddled by the question, the young pastor spoke of giving to the church as a personal matter between an individual and God, and encouraged the questioner to prayerfully consider the blessings he received and his ability to be generous. "No," the questioner interrupted the pastor. "I need to know how much I am supposed to give, what is expected. I can decide how to respond, but you have to tell me what I should give."

In the same way that one parishioner advised, "If you mean money, say money," another exclaimed, "If you want us to give, you have to ask!" People positively disposed to stewardship sermons report that they want to be asked to give. Leaving the question implicit might leave some listeners feeling a bit less uncomfortable, but most listeners find these sermons underwhelming. More than wanting to be asked to give, people also report that they appreciate clarity and specificity in the question. Asking people to "respond gratefully" or "give generously" is akin to asking them to be "more Christian." Everyone agrees that they should, but no one is quite sure what that means.

When the sermon concerns money and giving, what does the church really want people to give? Does the congregation's leadership want people to tithe, to grow in their giving, to give a certain amount, or to maintain their current level of giving? Do congregational leaders want people to remember to give in the weeks that they are not in worship? Do people need to understand that giving to special causes is in addition to and not in place of their regular offerings? The stewardship committee and congregational council often determine what they want people to give in response to the congregation's financial situation. "This is what we need to make budget." Or, "This is what we need to begin the day-care program." When congregational leaders determine what they want the congregation to give, the preacher should tell the congregation what has been decided.

Sometimes, congregations find that providing options is better than offering a single amount to give. One congregation asked everyone to give up one pizza a month and give the money to the church. The goal was 100 percent participation. "What about those of us who can afford only one pizza a month?" a few members asked. As congregational leaders realized that what they intended to be a small sacrifice was a real hardship for some of the faith community, they also realized that providing options would have been more helpful.

Yet, while asking for what is needed and providing options for giving might be good fund-raising, they do not make for good preaching. Because in preaching we ask people to give in response to God or the gospel, preachers, church boards, and finance and stewardship committees need to name the gospel or *good news* in giving. Generally speaking, the good news in giving is that giving is a way followers of Christ express our thanks and praise to God for the grace we have received, gratefully offer ourselves to God's service, and participate in God's own work in the world. Framing our giving as a response to and participation in God's own work is essential.

To get more specific, preachers and congregational leaders might ask, "How does what we are asking people to give further the gospel? What biblical story does what we are asking our congregation to give relate to? How can we ask using the language and images of Scripture?" Questions like these remind the preacher and church leaders that the specific and concrete things the church asks people to give, or the options the church provides, are never ends in themselves. They are ways we participate in something greater—"that is, in Christ God was reconciling the world to himself, not counting their trespasses against them, and entrusting the message of reconciliation to us" (2 Cor. 5:19). Asking how what we give furthers the gospel and relates to the Bible emboldens church leaders to say that what we give is part of God's plan of salvation, God's own work of recreating, reconciling, and righting us and the world, because what we give is a way we participate in the gospel.

Of course, to assert that what people give is a way they participate in God's own work of salvation means that what preachers and church leaders ask people to give is, in fact, an appropriate response to the gospel. This assertion requires, even demands, that we can articulate how what we ask people to give is part of God's plan of salvation. When we cannot name the good news in giving by saying how what we are asking for furthers God's reign, when what we ask for serves only to maintain the institution or to serve ourselves, we do better not to ask for it—at least as part of a sermon.

Experience reveals that the truth of Jesus's teaching about money is closer at hand than we sometimes realize. We often interpret the parable of the talents (Matt. 25:14–30) in terms of God's ultimate judgment on our use of our individual talents and abilities. This parable might also relate to the resources entrusted to congregations and faith communities and how they are used here and now. In one congregation, a woman stopped by the pastor's office and delivered a check for five thousand dollars "to further the congregation's ministry." Wanting to be prudent, the congregational council put the money in the bank to "save it for a rainy day." Several months later, the woman stopped by to see the pastor and ask what the congregation did with her gift. When the pastor told her that the council put it in the bank to save for the future, the woman responded, "I'm sorry to hear that. I wanted that money to make a difference, and I was going to give you another check. But I can keep my money in the bank." And the woman went away disappointed. In another congregation, the treasurer regularly boasted about how many months the building fund was ahead of the mortgage payments. "We have enough money to pay for the next sixteen months." When someone mentioned Jesus's parable of the rich fool (Luke 12:15–21), congregants connected the money in the building fund with the stuff accumulating in the rich fool's barns. The treasurer was dismayed when giving in general slowed.

When preachers and congregational leaders are convinced that what we are asking the congregation to give is a grateful response to and participation in God's own work in the world, we ask without apology, embarrassment, discomfort, or shame, because we trust God, "who by the power at work within us is able to accomplish abundantly far more than all we can ask or imagine" (Eph. 3:20). Preachers can then name the good news in giving, demonstrate trust in God, and exercise boldness that comes from the gospel when they craft sermons in which (1) exhortation follows and flows from gospel proclamation; (2) Jesus does the talking; and (3) people are invited rather than coerced or commanded.

Exhortation Follows Proclamation

I have long held that there is no one "canonical" form for a sermon—for example, three points and a poem, narrative, or scriptural exposition—and so have resisted offering formulae or recipes for crafting the homily. Following Fred Craddock, I invite preachers to fill their homiletic toolbox with sermon forms or designs that are "congenial not only to the gospel, but also to the ways human beings order, understand, and appropriate reality."[5] Preachers can then select the best tool for crafting a particular sermon in a way that gets the gospel message heard. So, for example, when students ask if it is good to use music videos in preaching, I generally respond, "Not at the senior living center."

Yet, as I listen to sermons, particularly stewardship sermons, I am increasingly aware of the truth of another of Fred Craddock's teachings. Craddock writes, "The form of a sermon is active, contributing to what the speaker wishes to say and do, sometimes no less persuasive than the content itself."[6] In many of the sermons that I hear, the form, structure, or movement of the sermon undermines the message. The common pattern in many of these sermons is to "save the best for last." In a fifteen-minute sermon, we get seven minutes of a problem or dilemma and how we are to blame for it followed by seven minutes of how we are to respond to make things better. Then, in the closing minute, the preacher tells us that we can do whatever it is that we need to do because God loves us, Jesus died and rose for us, and the Holy Spirit is with us. My problem with sermons constructed this way is that, after the roller-coaster ride from guilt to obligation, the gospel "proclamation" feels small, weak, and disconnected—even an afterthought. Were I to offer a formula or recipe for improving these sermons, it would be that the gospel proclamation be larger and come earlier in the sermon so that exhortation—in the case of stewardship, asking or inviting people to give—follows proclamation.

I acknowledge that my Lutheran bias toward God's grace is showing here. In the Small Catechism, Martin Luther explains the Third Article of the Apostles' Creed, which concerns the Holy Spirit, saying in part, "I believe that by my own understanding or strength I cannot believe in Jesus Christ my Lord or come to him, but instead the Holy Spirit has called me through the gospel, enlightened me with his gifts, made me holy and kept me in the true faith . . ."[7] As I listen to sermons that save the best for last, I find myself feeling overwhelmed and defeated by all that I am supposed to give and do, and find myself giving up before I ever get started. If I cannot believe in Jesus or come to him out of my own understanding and strength, how can I do all on my own whatever it is I am supposed to do to make the world better?

Lest one think this is a Lutheran's dilemma, Jana Childers, a Presbyterian minister who teaches preaching at San Francisco Theological Seminary, asserts that preaching attempts to open people to God before it attempts to get people to do anything else. Childers writes, "In some theological traditions, openness is regarded as the one thing human beings have to offer God; in others, God supplies even this. . . . To preach Jesus Christ is to allow God's word to work through one's personality and expressiveness in such a way that both preacher and congregation are opened."[8] Likewise, Mary Donovan Turner, a minister of the Christian Church (Disciples of Christ) who teaches preaching at the Pacific School of Religion in Berkeley, California, says that preaching disrupts life to create a space in which the Holy Spirit can work, a space in which the community can rethink, revisit priorities, or receive.[9]

Yet, I am most fond of the description of the relationship of proclamation and exhortation found in *Fulfilled in Your Hearing: The Homily in the Sunday Assembly*, the statement of the Bishops' Committee on Priestly Life and Ministry of the United States Conference of Catholic Bishops. *Fulfilled in Your Hearing* declares that, while the homily

> may well include evangelization, catechesis, and exhortation, . . . the homily is preached in order that a community of believers who have gathered to celebrate the liturgy [to worship] may do so more deeply and more fully—more faithfully—and thus be formed for Christian witness in the world.[10]

The preacher helps the congregation worship more deeply, fully, and faithfully by sharing

> the Christian vision of the world as the creation of a loving God. Into this world humans unleashed the powers of sin and death. These powers have been met, however, by God through his Son Jesus Christ, in whom he is at work not only to restore creation, but to transform it into a new heaven and a new earth.[11]

The statement asserts that hearing and accepting this vision of the world, this way of interpreting reality, requires a response.

Sometimes it will be appropriate to call people to repentance for the ways they have helped to spread the destructive powers of sin in the world. At other times, the preacher will invite the congregation to devote themselves to some specific action as a way of sharing in the redemptive and creative word of God. However, the response that is most general and appropriate "at all times and in every place" is the response of praise and thanksgiving.[12]

Walter Brueggemann contends that, "we must be summoned to an alternative imagination, in order that we might imagine the world and ourselves differently."[13] When the proclamation of the Christian vision of reality leaves people thanking and praising God, their response is one of gratitude. They imagine the world and themselves differently. They are eager and excited to give, to serve, to participate in what God is doing. Rather than saving the best for last, sermons, particularly stewardship sermons, should be constructed so that the gospel commands center stage and exhortation follows proclamation. Then, when it comes time to ask people to give, it is not so much the preacher asking as God inviting grateful people to participate in what God is doing. In fact, in sermons in which exhortation follows proclamation, preachers can dare to let the Lord God, Jesus, or the Holy Spirit do the talking.

Let Jesus Do the Talking

When preaching about money is grounded in the gospel, God, the prophet, or Jesus, rather than the preacher, speaks the first word. According to Scripture, Jesus has much to say about money, most of which preachers could not get away with saying themselves. Therefore, preachers do well to let Jesus do the talking. For example, preachers may not be able to say, "Our money defines us," but Jesus does. Jesus declares, "For where your treasure is, there your heart will be also" (Matt. 6:21). Even more pointedly, Jesus observes, "No one can serve two masters; for a slave will either hate the one and love the other, or be devoted to the one and despise the other. You cannot serve God and wealth" (Matt. 6:24). When a young man, who kept the commandments but still found himself lacking, asked Jesus what he must do to have eternal life, Jesus answered in terms of money: "If you wish to be perfect, go, sell your possessions, and give the money to the poor, and you will have treasure in heaven; then come, follow me" (Matt. 19:21). From Matthew's Gospel alone, we can see clearly that Jesus has opinions about how we relate to and what we do with our money.

Allowing God to speak to us through the Old Testament and epistles can be even more unsettling, even frightening. For example, what the Lord God declared through the prophet Amos is a valid indictment of American society's obsession with money: "Hear this, you that trample on the needy, and bring to ruin the poor of the land, saying, 'When will the new moon be over so that we may sell grain; and the sabbath, so that we may offer wheat for sale? We will make the ephah small and the shekel great, and practice deceit with false balances, buying the poor for silver and the needy for a pair of sandals, and selling the sweepings of the wheat.' The Lord has sworn by the pride of Jacob: 'Surely I will never forget any of their deeds'" (Amos 8:4–7). To a culture driven by consumption and the desire for more and more, the author of Hebrews exhorts, "Keep your lives free from the love of money, and be content with what you have; for he has said, 'I will never leave you or forsake you'" (13:5). The Epistle of James not only speaks to the futility of trusting our security to money, it also offers God's assessment:

> Come now, you rich people, weep and wail for the miseries that are coming to you. Your riches have rotted, and your clothes are moth-eaten. Your gold and silver have rusted, and their rust will be evidence against you, and it will eat your flesh like fire. You have laid up treasure for the last days. Listen! The wages of the laborers who mowed your fields, which you kept back by fraud, cry out, and the cries of the harvesters have reached the ears of the Lord of hosts. You have lived on the earth in luxury and in pleasure; you have fattened your hearts in a day of slaughter. You have condemned and murdered the righteous one, who does not resist you.
>
> James 5:1–6

When preachers allow the Lord God, Jesus, or the Holy Spirit to do the talking, they can say things that they could never say on their own. Of course, to do this, preachers listen to God speak to them before they ever utter a word to their congregations. By listening to God before and as they speak to the congregation, preachers stand (often uncomfortably) with their people under God's word, rather than standing with God's word against their people. The Lord God, Jesus, or the Holy Spirit can then address both the preacher and the hearers, who together try to understand and faithfully respond to what God is saying.

Invite Rather than Coerce or Command

When Jesus does the talking, the request to give is an invitation rather than a coercion or command. History shows how tempting commanding and coercing—appealing to obligation, fear, and guilt—can be. In 1873 John W. Pratt, a southern Presbyterian, wrote an essay that included a new phrase that would be used extensively for the next half century.[14] Pratt's essay was entitled, "Will a Christian Rob God?" For the next fifty years, the literature of Christian stewardship espoused the idea that the failure to give at least a tithe to the church was tantamount to robbing God. The key passage for this approach to giving is Malachi 3:8–10: "Will anyone rob God? Yet you are robbing me! But you say, 'How are we robbing you?' In your tithes and offerings! You are cursed with a curse, for you are robbing me—the whole nation of you! Bring the full tithe into the storehouse, so that there may be food in my house, and thus put me to the test, says the LORD of hosts; see if I will not open the windows of heaven for you and pour down for you an overflowing blessing." Withholding tithes and offerings to the church was understood as more than holding something back from a human institution, or expressing disapproval of the minister with one's checkbook. Not giving a tithe was, in effect, robbing the Lord God Almighty. God would curse those who withheld their tithes and pour down an overflowing blessing on those who gave. Of course, the whole of the tithe needed to be given to the church, or storehouse, which would distribute it. While this approach may have a scriptural basis, has been used by the church, and may be effective in certain circumstances, for many Christians, this approach is not consistent with the God revealed in Jesus Christ.

A preacher succumbing to the temptation to motivate people to give using methods inconsistent with the gospel is not confined to history. In my own preaching, as I undertake the challenge of getting congregations to give or respond financially, I can unintentionally slip into persuading, convincing, motivating, or cajoling people to do something. Parishioners sometimes want me to instruct, correct, decree, or direct—usually someone other than them. Threats, guilt, and shame may even become the motivating force of a message that, according to Paul, is supposed to be about God's reconciling love in Jesus Christ. I have learned to check the way I ask people to respond to ensure that it is consistent with the gospel. In this regard, I return again and again to an insight from Professor Charles Campbell, who teaches preaching at Duke Divinity School.

Professor Campbell asserts that Jesus embodies God's character and way of working in the world most specifically in his choice of preaching to announce the reign of God.[15] Both the form and the content of Jesus's preaching declare who God is and how God works in the world. By using preaching to announce God's reign, Jesus declares that God's way is neither silent passivity and acceptance nor coerced belief, forced agenda, and dominating control. By choosing preaching to proclaim God's reign, Jesus requires and demonstrates mutuality. Receiving the kingdom involves both the one speaking and the ones listening. Since he announces the reign of God by preaching, Jesus cannot force God's kingdom on anyone, because Jesus refuses to treat the listener as an object or commodity. In his preaching, Jesus does not coerce or control its outcome. Instead, Jesus's life and preaching allow humans the freedom of decision, choice, and expression. Although other approaches certainly would have guaranteed greater success, Jesus chose to work through preaching, rather than through overwhelming temptation or absolute constraints, in order to inaugurate God's reign.

Some might argue that Jesus's preaching is full of commands, if not coercion. In the Sermon on the Mount, for example, Jesus says, "You have heard that it was said, 'An eye for an eye and a tooth for a tooth.' But I say to you, Do not resist an evildoer. But if anyone strikes you on the right cheek, turn the other also; and if anyone wants to sue you and take your coat, give your cloak as well; and if anyone forces you to go one mile, go also the second mile" (Matt. 5:38–41). From Campbell's perspective, Jesus is not a commander issuing orders but a jester who has a fundamentally different perspective on the world and, through often comical antics, seeks to startle and dislocate people—especially those in power—so they might be released from their common-sense presuppositions and see and live in the world in new and creative ways.[16] Here, Jesus names the myth that violence is the ultimate solution to human conflict when he says, "You have heard it said. . . ." Then, with "But I say to you," Jesus puts on the cap and bells of the jester and invites us to imagine foolish alternatives to violent resistance—turn the other cheek, give your cloak as well as your coat, go the second mile.

Like the preaching of Jesus, the church's preaching of the gospel does not attempt to control people or to force an outcome. Rather, the church teaches and trusts that God is at work in preaching. In whatever ways we choose to ask people to give, preachers express their trust in the power of the gospel and God's involvement in the preaching endeavor by guaranteeing that the request to give does not cause people to feel commanded out of fear or coerced by the erroneous notion that God's love depends upon their actions. Instead, preachers imagine and describe or propose foolish alternatives to the way the world teaches us to regard and use money, alternatives that follow from the gospel. Preachers then invite their hearers to embrace and enter into those alternatives. In so doing, preaching speaks to people's best selves, appealing to them as God's children, those claimed by Christ, filled with the Holy Spirit, and empowered for service by God's grace.

Appeal to People's Best Selves

Preaching demands that preachers decide how they will approach the members of their congregations. Sermons are prepared and preached differently, depending on whether the preacher regards the members of the congregation as saints of God or considers them to be sinners. When the subject is money and giving, determining how to approach the congregation can become an easy, even subconscious decision. The way individual members and the congregation as a whole make decisions about money and use their financial resources gives the preacher plenty of evidence for judging the hearers as saints or sinners. At some point, preachers decide whether congregations are generous, whether they agree that money is a means and not an end, and whether congregations are concerned only with themselves or have a vision for something more. A preacher's assessment of these kinds of issues often gets expressed in the way sermons are structured and delivered. Rather than weighing the evidence and rendering a judgment, Jesus would have preachers use a different approach.

Paul reminds us of how Jesus approached us: "For while we were still weak, at the right time Christ died for the ungodly. . . . God proves his love for us in that while we still were sinners Christ died for us" (Rom. 5:6–8). Jesus's action invites preachers to regard their hearers, first and foremost, as those for whom Christ died. Preachers will then approach their congregations as God's beloved children. We will strive not to hold people's attitudes and actions about money and giving, which compete with and contradict the gospel, against them. In both the form and the delivery of the sermon, we will appeal to people's best selves.

Appealing to people's best selves does not mean ignoring or over-looking stinginess, ingratitude, preoccupation with money, or concern only for the self. However, rather than chastising people, preachers appeal to their best selves when we assume that most people care about others and want to give and explore what keeps them from giving. Are people struggling to make ends meet? Are they afraid of not having sufficient financial resources for the future? Is their self-worth somehow tied up in their financial status? Some parishioners report that the most helpful sermons are those in which the preacher authentically address-es the struggles to be generous givers and faithful stewards.

One way that preachers can appeal to their hearers' best selves is to name the struggle between being consumers and children of God. Kirsten L. Fryer, associate pastor of Peace Lutheran Church in Wauna-kee, Wisconsin, names this struggle by inviting her hearers into Jesus's encounter with a man who, on the one hand, wanted to inherit eternal life and, on the other, "was shocked and went away [from Jesus] griev-ing, for he had many possessions" (Mark 10:22). Pastor Fryer entitles her sermon, which follows, "People of Word and Stuff."[17]

PEOPLE OF WORD AND STUFF

One of my friends told me last weekend that his two-week-old nephew is the owner of an iPod shuffle. As I reflect on the conver-sation, perhaps the most disturbing thing is that my mind immedi-ately went to an ad I see every week on my drive. The rainbow of iPods immediately flashed in my mind. I didn't ask, "Why on earth does a newborn need an iPod?" I asked, "What color does he have?"

From a very young age, we are bombarded with words and words and words—ads on TV, along the road, on the radio, in our magazines, online, and even on city buses. According to the National Institute on Media and the Family, the average American child may view as many as 40,000 television commercials every year. Children as young as three can recognize brand logos, and brand loyalty may start as young as age two.[18] In spite of the fact that young children can't even distinguish between advertising and television programs, billions of dollars are spent every year in an attempt to "sell" products to young people. And that doesn't even include the loads of money spent to convince us, the grown-ups, that we need the stuff that the advertisers sell.

It wouldn't be such a problem except for the fact that we pay attention to the ads. We let them convince us that we need more and more and more stuff. And we like our stuff. And that's okay. I like having clothes and books and pots to cook with. I type my sermons on my computer and correspond over e-mail and Facebook with many friends and family. But I—and I suspect many of us—have to be careful. We have to be careful because it is really easy to begin to let all of that stuff define who we are. It is really tempting to let all of that stuff shape our identities.

I know this is the reason that today's Gospel reading [Mark 10:17–31] is so hard for me to hear. Like the man in the Gospel, I don't typically have trouble obeying the commandments, "You shall not murder; you shall not commit adultery; you shall not steal; you shall not bear false witness; you shall not defraud; honor your father and mother." What is hard for me, and I suspect most of us in this room, is what comes next: "You lack one thing; go, sell what you own, and give the money to the poor, and you will have treasure in heaven; then come, follow me." Most of us, like this man, have many possessions. And the thought of selling all of them and giving the money to the poor is pretty much out of the question. We *need* those things, don't we?

You don't need to raise your hands, but who in this room has dreamed about a nicer car, a bigger house? Has anyone ever imagined that maybe, if you had this or that new gizmo, that maybe you'd be happier? Have you looked with envy on your neighbor's new toy and felt like they were better than you because of their possession? We've all, to some extent, done these things. We live in a consumer driven society. We are shaped and molded to consume . . . to the point of consuming twice as much as Americans did fifty years ago. And yet, even with more stuff, for Americans, national happiness peaked sometime in the 1950s.[19] We have more stuff, yet we are less happy and more in debt. And yet, it is so tempting to think that maybe just one more thing will make us happy, will shape our identity in a more positive light, will make us better people.

We are bombarded by words and stuff. Our identities have become molded and shaped by what we own. And the thought of giving all that stuff up probably makes us a little bit sick to our stomachs. All of it? Not just the stuff that is worn out and no good to us anymore? Yes, Jesus tells the man to sell his possessions. Everything. Not just the Goodwill pile, but all of it. And the man, much like most of us here, goes away shocked and grieving, "for he had many possessions."

Even in an age before iPods, SUVs, and billions of dollars a year spent on advertising, Jesus knew that it is so easy to let our stuff define our identities. He knew how tempting it is to be shaped by the many words we hear telling us we need more and more and more. He knows that all too often, we are people whose identities are reduced to a few words and wrapped up in stuff.

Jesus tells the man to sell his stuff, not his identity. Jesus does not ask him, or us, to sell our identities as people of words and stuff. The identity, after all, that Christ gives us is indeed one of stuff and of Word. It is an identity that is given to us because of the very material stuff of the water of Baptism, the bread and the wine of Eucharist, all connected with the very real Word of God. We are people whose identities are very much wrapped up in stuff and in Word. But we are not bound by Word and by stuff; we are freed because of it.

Our identity in Christ cannot be bought or sold. This identity can only be given as a gracious gift by God, not because of anything we have done to earn it or purchase it or deserve it, but simply because we are God's people, who, in Luther's words, are "purchased and freed from our sins, from death, and the power of the devil, not with gold or silver but with Christ's holy, precious blood and with his innocent suffering and death."[20] We are loved because of who we are and not because of what we do or do not own.

Jesus calls us to "belong to him, live under him in his kingdom, and serve him in eternal righteousness, innocence, and blessedness."[21] And because of this identity, we can give generously. We can live as good stewards of our money, our time, and our talents. It is because of this identity as people shaped by water, bread and wine, together with God's Word that we can even begin to contemplate the possibility that maybe we don't need all of the other stuff that threatens to take over and overshadow the identity that can not be taken away, the identity that cannot be bought or sold.

When we get caught up in identities shaped by the need for more and more and more stuff, identities molded by an endless babble of words telling us that we need more, our lives are forever driven by the need to consume, the need to earn, the need to buy. Our identities become centered upon what we have. It is so easy to forget who we are. And sometimes, even easier to forget whose we are.

Let me remind you today: you are a child of God. Look around you. These people, your friends and neighbors, are your family. They, too, are children of God. We are God's stuff, molded and shaped by a gracious and loving creator. And we, the people of God, are signed and sealed by the Holy Spirit; we are marked with the cross of Christ forever. This identity does not come without burdens. It does not free us from responsibility; it even demands that we give up and give away. It is an identity into which we spend our whole lives growing and struggling. But this identity comes with loads and loads of grace. This identity, which we cannot buy, sell, or earn, comes with a promise. To God's people, through Word and through water, bread, and wine, God gives an identity and a promise of abundant and everlasting life. Amen.

In Conclusion

Did you find yourself in this sermon? Did you experience God's good news? Jesus gives us an identity based on God's word of promise and the stuff of water, bread, and wine. Only after we receive this good news does the preacher invite us to embrace this identity by contemplating the possibility that we do not need all of the other stuff that threatens to take over and overshadow our identity as God's children, an identity that cannot be bought or sold. Trusting that we are God's children, we can generously give up our money and give our possessions away. The invitation to give flows from the gospel. Breaking open God's Word in this way, to discover the good news, is the theme of the next three chapters.

AS YOU PREPARE YOUR SERMON . . .

- In the sermons that you preach and hear, what is the answer to the question, why should people give to the church? Is that answer more preaching or fund-raising? Why?

- How does what you are asking people to give relate to and further the gospel? What biblical story or image best fits with what you are asking for?

- How explicit is the request to give in the sermons you hear and preach? What form does the request take—implication, invitation, command, or something else?

- Based on the sermons that you hear and preach, how would you describe the congregation being addressed as stewards or as givers?

CHAPTER 3

What Does
the Bible Say?

VISIBLY TERRIFIED by the idea that the pastor would actually preach about money and giving, and that the congregation would then ask people to pledge, Harriet, an officer on the church board, sat flipping furiously through the pages of her Bible. "It's right there," she declared at last with a sigh of relief. "Jesus said it: 'But when you give alms, do not let your left hand know what your right hand is doing, so that your alms may be done in secret; and your Father who sees in secret will reward you'" (Matt. 6:3–4). Then, providing her own commentary on the text, Harriet declared, "Pastor, sermons about money, and asking people to tell what they are going to give, are *not* what Jesus wants."

Is that really what the Bible says? If not, what does the Bible say about money and giving? And how do we know? Or, more realistically, how do we decide? In preaching especially, it is essential that preachers make a claim about what the Bible says about money and giving—or whatever we mean by stewardship. New Testament scholar David Bartlett unabashedly declares that "right preaching is the interpretation of Scripture." According to Professor Bartlett, while excellent Christian speech might entertain, inform, inspire, and offer opinions in ways that help the faithful and edify the community, "unless [the sermon] is an interpretation of the text or texts that the congregation has just heard read aloud, it is not preaching."[1] As Christian preaching, sermons about stewardship—money and giving—grow out of and are governed by the Scriptures read in worship.

What does the Bible say about money and giving? It is a difficult question to answer unequivocally. For starters, as I said in chapter 1, while God is unquestionably concerned about money and how we use it, the Bible includes a variety of perspectives on what we are to do with what we have. In fact, as with so many subjects, the church in North America historically combed the Scriptures to find a biblical basis for what it wanted or needed to do to generate money for the church, as Christians all over the world have done throughout the church's history. In some times and places, the church commanded people to tithe. At other times and in other places, the church reflected our council member Harriet and advocated keeping giving secret. In the process, many biblical perspectives emerged. Cheerful giving, giving to God first, and tithing are but a few. So we cannot name a single biblical approach and perspective, and many seasoned preachers know the dangers of trying. More than being scripturally dishonest, sermons that offer a single, air-tight approach arouse the congregation's suspicions, cause them to feel manipulated, and usually backfire because of how they respond. I have become suspicious when congregants tell preachers that they want to hear what the Bible says about money and giving, or anything else for that matter. In my experience, they may be saying that the preacher needs to proclaim the biblical perspective they agree with and think others need to hear and subscribe to.

What does the Bible say about money and giving? Because I cannot offer a single, simple, straightforward answer, in this chapter I offer six principles to guide and govern how we use the Bible to preach about money and giving. These guidelines include (1) proclaiming God's promise in giving, (2) giving voice to all the Bible has to say, (3) employing a consistent exegetical procedure, (4) standing with God's people, (5) taking Scripture seriously, and (6) untangling biblical perspectives. In the next three chapters, I then attempt to untangle biblical perspectives on money and giving by offering scriptural reflections on why, how, and what we give. In the discussion of the Bible in chapters 3 through 6, my thinking about biblical perspectives on money and giving is indebted to the work of Mark Allan Powell, who teaches New Testament at Trinity Lutheran Seminary, Columbus, Ohio,[2] and conversations with Timothy V. Olson, a pastor with a background in banking and congregational stewardship, who regularly preaches in the manner I suggest in this book, and had been doing so long before I ever suggested it.

Even though I long to provide straightforward answers to why, how, and what we give, as a steward entrusted by the church to care for and attend to the preaching of the gospel, I know the principles that govern preachers' use of the Bible in preaching about money and giving—and everything else—are more important than whatever biblical perspective(s) we embrace to answer the questions about giving to God. For me, the most important biblical principle is proclaiming God's promise in giving.

Proclaim God's Promise in Giving

In chapter 2, I encouraged preachers to name the good news in giving or name how giving is a response to the gospel. Preachers do this best when we proclaim God's promises related to giving time, talent, and treasure. Preachers learn to proclaim God's promise by looking for what God is doing as we reflect upon and study Scripture. Powell observes that, because the Bible contains a lot of commandments, many of which concern how people of faith use our money, we may instinctively look for what we are supposed to do with our money and conclude that God's expectations are so high that we will never be able to measure up. Our temptation, therefore, is to avoid or downplay this biblical topic as we accept our imperfections with varying degrees of denial and discomfort.[3]

A better approach is to look for and preach about God's promises related to money and giving—"promises designed to inspire our confidence rather than arouse our guilt."[4] In all preaching, preachers cultivate the discipline of proclaiming God's promise by opening the Bible and instinctively looking for what God is up to, what Jesus is doing, or how the Spirit is blowing, rather than what we are supposed to do, how we are expected to act, and what it means for us to be faithful. After all, God, not humanity, is the star of Scripture, and to make us the center of God's Word is its own form of idolatry. The people who listen to sermons understand this. While professional religious leaders automatically look to Scripture to discover how we are to emulate Jesus, the people in the pews are smarter. They know Jesus is Jesus and we, well, we are us. Most of us are not willing to do crucifixion and we have not figured out how to do resurrection for ourselves. So, as I said in chapter 1, people want to know who God is, what God is like, and what Jesus is

up to before preachers tell them how God expects us to live or the ways
God tells us to behave or what we are supposed to do with money.

Looking for what God or Jesus is doing in Mark's account of the man
who asked Jesus what he must do to inherit eternal life (Mark 10:17–23)
takes the spotlight off of what many correctly consider Jesus's impossible command to "sell what you own, and give the money to the poor,
and you will have treasure in heaven." Instead, the key to the passage is
"Jesus, looking at him, loved him" (Mark 10:21). Rather than issuing an
unachievable order, Jesus loved this man so much that he helped him
to see the impossibility of trying to save oneself. In love, Jesus invited
this man to let go of the "many possessions" that stood between him
and God. Then Jesus declared God's promise: "How hard it will be for
those who have wealth to enter the kingdom of God! . . . For mortals
it is impossible, but not for God; for God all things are possible" (Mark
10:23, 27).

When people of faith, and preachers in particular, look for what
God is doing in Scripture, we understand that we can keep the stewardship "commandments" in the Bible empowered by and in response
to what God has done, is doing, and will do for us, humanity and all
creation—loving, guiding, guarding, and blessing. Preachers—and the
whole church—can then proclaim God's promise in giving.

Give Voice to All That the Bible Has to Say

In many congregations, the preaching task sometime during October
and November is to preach the Bible, the New Testament, or at least the
appointed or selected readings from a "stewardship perspective." Frequently, this means that preachers need to fit, even force, money and
giving into a sermon when these topics are needed, in essence preaching
the Bible from the perspective of money. Often preachers do this in one
of two ways. Many preachers report that, feeling the pressure to entice
people to give, they set aside seriously exploring a biblical perspective
on money and giving and attempt to say something likely to generate
needed results. Alternatively, preachers might select a preaching text
that provides a single perspective likely to do the trick. Preachers admit
they often feel uncomfortable approaching the stewardship sermon in
these ways, and so set money and giving aside until the next year. The
congregation is left with a single perspective in a single sermon. So, for

example, a congregation might never hear about tithing because the preacher or congregational leaders fear that a sermon about tithing on Stewardship Sunday will anger or overwhelm people to such a degree that they will not give more money.

Rather than preaching a single sermon in which the subject of money and giving might be forced or slanted to generate immediate results, a better approach is to give voice to all that the Bible has to say about money and giving. This is how the church proclaims Jesus. The church does not make Jesus smaller by, for example, selecting one of the four Gospels—Matthew, Mark, Luke, or John—as our single, scriptural portrait of Jesus. We use all four Gospels to proclaim Jesus, along with the epistles and portions of the Old Testament. In this same way, employing the breadth and depth of Scripture to preach about money and giving expands and enriches faith and understanding in at least three ways.

First, preaching all that the Bible has to say by using many different passages over time, rather than a single verse or story on a single occasion, makes the topic bigger and more significant. More than considering the immediate question of how one will respond to a single scriptural perspective on money and giving, giving voice to all that the Bible has to say frees the pastor and congregation to consider the more foundational question of how money, wealth, and material possessions relate to faith, discipleship, and the reign of God. In this way, Scripture helps both the preacher and the faithful distinguish between stewardship and fund-raising. Giving voice to all the Bible has to say is in keeping with the truth that proclamation and conversation about giving money to the church in response to the gospel is bigger and more complex than providing an answer that people might disagree with or a course of action that they may be unable or unwilling to follow. Preaching all that the Bible has to say empowers people to connect the resources of their faith with the realities of their financial and material lives as they seek to live faithfully in response to the gospel.

Second, when preachers give voice to all that the Bible has to say, they will inevitably preach about money and giving more often, particularly at times other than the annual stewardship campaign. People can then consider possibilities without feeling pressured to make an immediate response. So, for example, a preacher and congregation might use a sermon or a sermon series to explore the blessings of tithing at a time in the year when the preacher does not need to ask the congregation to tithe and the congregation does not need to decide immediately how to respond to the preacher's question. Preachers are blessed with a certain freedom, even boldness on those occasions. People have time to reflect, pray, and allow the words of Scripture to sink in and stick with them. Perhaps this is why some congregants observe that, sometimes, the best preaching about money and giving occurs when the pastor is not asking members to increase their giving.

Third, when preachers preach all the Bible has to say, it is more likely that, over time, something the Bible says will speak to everyone in the congregation. In a sense, we give the Holy Spirit more to work with. For example, some might resonate with the invitation to give God first fruits rather than leftovers. Others might be eager for an invitation to tithe. If we preach only a single perspective, we miss one—or perhaps both—of these groups. We may even be tempted to look for a lowest common denominator so as not to "somehow become a stumbling block to the weak" (1 Cor. 8:9), with the result that we serve baby food to those who have an appetite for giving and so desire a steak dinner of a sermon.

Preachers who follow the lectionary—the system of Scripture readings appointed for worship on a given day or occasion—rather than selecting their own sermon texts advise that the best way to preach all that the Bible has to say is to let the lectionary be your friend. Instead of allowing the calendar of the annual stewardship campaign or the congregation's financial situation determine when money gets addressed from the pulpit, they preach about money and giving whenever money is part of any of the appointed Scripture readings heard in worship. Sermons about money and giving flow from the lectionary and are not imposed upon the Scripture read in worship. Preachers can honestly say that Jesus or the greater church determines when the subject of money gets addressed, as well as what gets said. They can point to the readings and truthfully say that, on this occasion, to preach biblically is to preach about money.

Preachers who do not follow the lectionary, and especially those responsible for selecting the preaching text, report that they garner some of these same benefits by exercising this prerogative and responsibility of selecting the preaching text in conversation with congregational leaders and even the congregation, so that determining the readings read and heard in worship is a communal act, even if only implicitly. Some preachers, both those who follow the lectionary readings and those who select Scripture in community, go so far as to allow the readings heard in worship rather than the congregation's budgeting process, to determine both the timing and the form of the annual stewardship campaign.

Employ a Consistent Exegetical Procedure

People need to trust that the preacher approaches, studies, and interprets the Bible in sermons about stewardship, money, and giving in the same way that the preacher proclaims the Bible in other sermons and, indeed, in other areas of life. Both the way Scripture read in worship is selected for the stewardship sermon and how those readings are interpreted must be consistent with the approach the preacher uses the rest of the year. Changing the way the Scripture read in worship is chosen introduces an element of curiosity or even suspicion. What questions might the congregation have when they discover that their preacher, who never deviates from the Revised Common Lectionary, set the lectionary aside on Stewardship Sunday and selected the preaching text herself? They might wonder whether their pastor is justifying an agenda rather than listening to God. Even preachers charged with selecting the sermon text report that they need to be prayerful and careful, so members of their congregations do not wonder whether they are choosing Scripture without the Spirit's help. Questions like these and the underlying skepticism they represent can lead some listeners to discount and resist the message. Therefore, preachers best use the same method for selecting the Scripture readings for Stewardship Sunday that they use the rest of the year.

More important, the exegetical method used to interpret passages about money and giving must be the same procedure the preacher ordinarily uses. Preachers cannot, for example, argue that Leviticus 27:32— "All tithes of herd and flock, every tenth one that passes under the shepherd's staff, shall be holy to the LORD"—is a divine command binding upon us and then, a few months later, argue that we need to understand Leviticus 18:22—"You shall not lie with a male as with a woman; it is an abomination"—in its cultural context and let our interpretation be informed by the American Psychological Association, which has taken the position that people should not be told that they can change their sexual orientation through therapy. People attentive to both sermons will rightfully ask how we claim some verses from Leviticus as God's eternal command while dismissing others as no longer relevant.

I am not advocating here any particular procedure for interpreting Scripture—though I do have much to say about interpreting the Bible for preaching elsewhere.[5] Christians agree that the Bible is God's Word, that Scripture is meaningful and important for their lives, and that they take it very seriously. Christians are also clear that what they agree on about the Bible far exceeds what they disagree about it. Yet, especially on issues like money and giving, which cut close to home, faithful people in the same congregation read and interpret Scripture many different ways. For some, a given passage from the Bible is history; every word is literally true. For others, it is a prescription or command that we are to follow. Still others will read the passage as a model of how God interacts with the world and us. Some Christians read Scripture for inspiration, rather than for information. Others look to the Bible for a perspective or frame of reference on the world and Christian life. Still others read Scripture as a testimony to God's saving activity, a conversation partner, or even a conversation itself.[6] In fact, some argue that the most pressing issue facing the church today is how we read and interpret the Bible.

Regardless of how they and their congregants understand the Bible, all preachers have—or should have—a procedure for selecting and interpreting Scripture for preaching that is appropriate to their understanding of the nature of Scripture and the biblical material being explored and that is congenial to their own process of understanding.[7] Fred Craddock argues, "It is vital that one's procedure lead smoothly into and through a text and that it be simple to be followed almost unconsciously."[8] Whatever the kind or topic of the sermon, preachers are obliged to ask how the Scriptures authorize the sermon and to ensure that the Bible is used honestly and with integrity. In sermons on money and giving, the procedure employed must be consistent with the preacher's established pattern or practice. Preachers are therefore careful to check against approaching and interpreting the Bible differently in the stewardship sermon than they do in other areas of their preaching ministry.

Stand with Your People

Nora Tubbs Tisdale, who teaches preaching at Yale Divinity School, advises that, when preaching prophetically—which, I hasten to add, sermons on money and giving frequently are in a consumer-driven culture—preachers stand with their people under God's Word, rather than with God's Word against their people.[9] Old Testament scholar Walter Brueggemann observes that the opposite often happens. Brueggemann asserts that, when most congregations struggle with biblical interpretation, three voices are operative: the voice of the biblical text, the voice of the preacher, and the voice of the congregation. Far too often, Brueggemann says, pastors team up with the texts to "triangle" against their congregations in preaching, leaving the congregation "a hostile, resistant outsider." Brueggemann contends that it is better for the preacher to stand with the congregation against the text, letting God's Word offend them both.[10]

Consider how a preacher crafts and delivers a sermon on portions of the Sermon on the Mount when she or he stands with the congregation and listens to Jesus speak to them all. "Jesus said to his disciples, 'Truly I tell you, it will be hard for a rich person to enter the kingdom of heaven. Again I tell you, it is easier for a camel to go through the eye of a needle than for someone who is rich to enter the kingdom of God.' When the disciples heard this, they were greatly astounded and said, 'Then who can be saved?'" (Matt. 19:23–25). Both preacher and congregation will have a completely different experience of this reading when the preacher joins the gathering of disciples in listening to and reacting to Jesus, instead of presuming to speak for Jesus.

When we stand with our people under God's Word, we listen to the Bible before—and more than—we speak for the Bible. We acknowledge the ways the Bible challenges and convicts us. We construct sermons using forms and language that make clear to our hearers that we are listening with them to what God's Word has to say. For example, preachers use the pronoun *us* rather than *you*, as in, "God wants us . . ." Even more, we name shared struggles, fears, questions, objections, and concerns. Sermons need to speak for the people to God as well as to the people from God. When preachers stand with their people under God's Word, they are better able to do both.

Take the Bible Seriously

For preachers and congregations to credibly preach and teach that the Bible is the foundation and guide for using money faithfully and giving in response to the gospel, the congregation must take the Bible seriously. Preachers, congregational leaders, and people who regularly listen to sermons report that, when people experience a discrepancy or a disconnection between what they hear in the sermon and experience in the congregation, people trust their own experience more than the preacher's words.[11] So, if a congregation wants members to take the Bible seriously, its leaders will take the Bible seriously and will teach everyone in the congregation to take the Bible seriously.

Perhaps the most important way a congregation can demonstrate the seriousness it affords Scripture is for the congregation to follow the same biblical approach to money and giving with its own finances that it asks members of the congregation to use. So, for example, when the congregation teaches that God, through the church, should receive the first fruits of our labor, then the first disbursements the congregation makes ought to be for benevolence and ministries beyond the congregation, thereby giving its own first fruits to God. People notice when congregations teach one thing and do another. For example, one congregation liked to use what it called "a body of Christ" motif and then divide the budget by the number of "members" to determine its giving. To be consistent, understanding itself as a member of the body of Christ invited this congregation to divide the diocesan budget by the number of member congregations and give accordingly. When congregational leaders did not follow through on this approach, members noticed. To be consistent, congregations that instruct members to tithe will give a tenth of their income away.

Some parishioners and even congregational leaders might attempt to change the focus from how the congregation allocates its money to whether the preacher's financial habits are biblical. The preacher is certainly a primary example and witness to biblical stewardship, most notably because some people will use the preacher's inability to measure up as an excuse for them not to try. Yet, more important to most churchgoers than how the preacher spends her or his money is the way the congregation spends its money. When the church asks people to give biblically, whatever that means, people will watch to see whether the church does.

Untangle Biblical Perspectives

Last, to authentically, clearly, and consistently preach sermons about money and giving that grow out of Scripture, preachers and congregational leaders must answer the question of what the Bible says about money and giving for themselves and their hearers at a particular time in a congregation's life. Moreover, preachers need to be able to point to the passages where the Bible speaks to these subjects. A pastor once told me that, when the local industry was booming and people's incomes grew year after year, it was appropriate to teach people to honor God by "contributing a freewill offering in proportion to the blessing that you have received from the LORD your God" (Deut. 16:10). When the company downsized and people lost their jobs, the congregation needed to look at money and giving differently.

If preachers are not careful, we might unintentionally combine biblical approaches to money and giving in the same way that we mix the accounts of Jesus's birth in the Gospels so that the magi (Matt. 2:1–12) arrive at the manger alongside the shepherds (Luke 2:1–20), an event not recorded in Scripture. To conflate biblical perspectives on money and giving by, for example, asking people to cheerfully give a tithe of first fruits and then grow in their giving creates an approach to giving that may sound biblical but cannot be found in Scripture. A more authentic and effective approach is to select one perspective—giving cheerfully, giving first fruits, tithing, or growing in giving—and clearly teach and emphasize it in the stewardship sermon or campaign, the occasion or time of year when the congregation explicitly asks people to give or grow in their giving to the church.

Preachers may need to untangle the distinct biblical perspectives and approaches to money and giving found in (or invented from) the Bible and, together with congregational leaders, determine which one(s) to emphasize in both preaching and the congregation's stewardship programming and communication. As I said, the church does not have a single, eternal, divinely instituted practice of stewardship. We cannot name or claim *the* single biblical perspective on money or scriptural precedent for giving. Rather, the Bible includes multiple perspectives and precedents, which can be organized and reconfigured in numerous ways. I find it helpful to consider what the Bible says about money and giving in terms of why we give, how we give, and what we give. I consider these questions in the next three chapters.

AS YOU PREPARE YOUR SERMON . . .

- Do the sermons you preach and hear about money and giving emphasize God's promise more than our responsibility? How can you tell? Which side of the coin do you think the sermons should emphasize? Why?

- In the course of a year, how often do you preach or hear sermons about money and giving? Because money is such an important part of our lives, what do you make of how often you preach or hear sermons on this topic?

- How does the interpretation of Scripture in the stewardship sermon compare with the way Scripture is interpreted in other sermons? How can you tell?

- In the sermons that you preach and hear, would you say that the preacher stands with the people under God's Word or with God's Word against the people? Why would you say this?

- In the way it spends its money, how seriously does your congregation take the Bible? Why do you say this?

CHAPTER 4

Why Does the Bible Say We Give?

"WHY DO WE GIVE money to the church?" a child asks her mother, who is filling Sunday's offering envelope. How will the mother answer her daughter's question? How do we answer this question for our children? How does the preacher answer this question for us? Do we say that we give to help pay the church's bills? Do we say that we give because of all the good things the church does—teaching children, standing for the best things in the community, fostering happiness and human welfare, providing help and friendship, and caring for people in need? How about answering by reciting a Bible verse or telling a Bible story? What verse would we choose? What story would we tell?

Whatever verse or story we pick, the Bible tells us that our giving is an expression of something bigger and more profound than our church. In terms of money and giving, Scripture's greatest gift is to keep before us the reason we give to God. We give to God in response to all that God has given us—particularly in the life, death, and resurrection of Jesus—and as a way of sharing in God's own will for and work in the world. In other words, we give in response to the gospel. According to the Bible, we give to God (1) as an act of worship, (2) as a way of participating in God's reign, (3) as an act of resistance, (4) as a way of bearing witness, and (5) to grow in grace. Some preachers also believe that the Bible teaches that we give (6) to receive. Individuals and even congregations are motivated to give for various reasons. Therefore, while preachers might select a particular scriptural reason to give for the annual stewardship sermon, we will also appropriately include all of these biblical reasons for giving as we preach over time.

An Act of Worship

People of faith offer our gifts as part of the Sunday service because we give to God as *an act of worship*. At their best, our offerings are like the gift of an unnamed woman of whom Jesus said, "Truly I tell you, wherever the good news is proclaimed in the whole world, what she has done will be told in remembrance of her" (Mark 14:9). Mark reports that as Jesus sat at table in the house of Simon the leper at Bethany, "a woman came with an alabaster jar of very costly ointment of nard, and she broke open the jar and poured the ointment on his head" (Mark 14:3). In accounts of giving in the Old Testament, this unnamed woman in Mark's Gospel, and pilgrims visiting holy places today, we see that worshipers bring things they value to God's altar and leave them there as an expression of their love, adoration, and devotion to God or Christ. The woman poured out "an alabaster jar of very costly ointment of nard." In the Old Testament, the gift might be grain, "drink offerings," birds, or small animals. Today, pilgrims might offer themselves or leave jewelry, letters, flowers, mementos of loved ones, or other cherished possessions.

Mark Allan Powell observes, "Most of us know what it is like to love someone so much that we want to give them things."[1] We do not give because we should or are obliged to; we give because we want to. We experience joy, even excitement, in giving gifts to people we love. When we give to God as an act of worship, we give out of glad and generous hearts as an expression of love and devotion to the God who is so good to us. We make God, rather than ourselves, the center of our devotion. We deny ourselves, giving up something that we value, sacrificing our desires and our needs. When we give as an act of worship, thanks and praise replace self-interest and guilt.

Often, the gifts we give to those we love are not very practical. This is why some who saw the woman anointing Jesus became angry and scolded her. From their perspective, the ointment was being wasted. These people felt the ointment should have been sold and the money given to the poor (Mark 14:4–5). In the Old Testament, the offerings were destroyed. Today, pilgrims' offerings are simply left on the altar and, when the altar becomes too full, they are collected and stored or sometimes displayed.

For those giving as an act of worship, how the things they offer would be used, whether to provide for the church or help the poor or for some other worthy cause, is an afterthought, if they give it any thought at all. They understand the offering in Sunday worship as a holy opportunity to show their love for and devotion to God by giving up something they value—money. As we place an envelope into the offering plate, our words of thanks and praise are joined by our actions in an act of worship that is both simple and sincere.

Participation in God's Mission

For those concerned about what will become of their gifts, Scripture indicates that we give to *participate in the mission, reign, or kingdom of God*. In *When God Speaks through You: How Faith Convictions Shape Preaching and Mission*, I reflect on the commissions that the Gospel writers report Jesus gave to the church. These commissions include (1) making disciples, (2) taking up our cross and following, (3) forgiving and reconciling, (4) worshiping God, (5) loving one another, and (6) proclaiming the nearness of God's reign.[2] I understand these scriptural charges as variations on the vision of Jesus's preaching ministry, which I describe as "fulfillment."[3] "Jesus came to Galilee, proclaiming the good news of God, and saying, 'The time is fulfilled, and the kingdom of God has come near; repent, and believe in the good news'" (Mark 1:14–15).

The promises of Scripture that Jesus fulfills and the long-promised reign of God, which Jesus brings near, certainly have a monetary dimension. This is nowhere more apparent than in the Gospel of Luke.[4] According to Luke, Jesus is on the side of the poor. In the Magnificat, Mary says, "[God] has filled the hungry with good things, and sent the rich away empty" (Luke 1:53). In his inaugural sermon at Nazareth, Jesus declared that the Lord anointed him to bring good news to the poor (Luke 4:18). Luke tells us that Jesus was himself poor; he and his disciples received financial support from a group of Galilean women, who continued to support them when Jesus went up to Jerusalem for the last days of his life.[5] When Jesus sent the Twelve out to proclaim the kingdom of God and to heal, Jesus made them poor and dependent when he instructed them, "Take nothing for your journey, no staff, nor bag, nor bread, nor money—not even an extra tunic" (Luke 9:1–3).

Jesus called the poor "blessed" because the kingdom of God belongs to them (Luke 6:20). Wealth and possessions pose a radical danger to

Christian discipleship, so the rich share in the kingdom of God—or are banished from it—by virtue of how they treat the poor and needy. As Jesus tells it, while a poor man named Lazarus sat with Abraham in the life to come, a rich man's treatment of Lazarus in this life landed him a chasm away (Luke 16:19–31). While the ultimate hope of the poor is the coming eschatological reversal, their hope in the present is the fellowship of a new community, where justice, equality, and compassion are living realities. The community of believers is to be the place in the world where the good news of God's love for the poor, embodied most fully in Jesus, is transformed into practical reality. Luke calls Jesus's followers not to totally abandon our possessions but to use them as a means of discipleship—placing our possessions at the service of those in need in a radical way. So, for example, Zacchaeus's standard is "half . . . to the poor" (Luke 19:8).

The Acts of the Apostles presents the New Testament church as the kind of community that Jesus envisioned. According to Acts, "All who believed were together and had all things in common; they would sell their possessions and goods and distribute the proceeds to all, as any had need. . . . No one claimed private ownership of any possessions, but everything they owned was held in common. . . . There was not a needy person among them, for as many as owned lands or houses sold them and brought the proceeds of what was sold. They laid it at the apostles' feet, and it was distributed to each as any had need" (Acts 2:44–45; 4:32–35). Later in the New Testament, voluntary giving replaces holding all things in common. Yet, concern for the poor remains a characteristic of the Christian community. The author of James writes, "Religion that is pure and undefiled before God, the Father, is this: to care for orphans and widows in their distress, and to keep oneself unstained by the world" (James 1:27). This writer asks, "If a brother or sister is naked and lacks daily food, and one of you says to them, 'Go in peace; keep warm and eat your fill,' and yet you do not supply their bodily needs, what is the good of that?" (James 2:15–16).

Paul Galbreath, who teaches Christian worship at Union Seminary in Richmond, Virginia, observes, "From the earliest days, Christian communities were known for their hospitality and care for the poor. Neighbors wondered what caused these Christians to care for widows and orphans, visit the sick, and take food to those in prison."[6] Christians' response to the needs of those around them set them apart and made them both a curiosity and an attraction. Giving and spending money to provide for the material needs of others is a chief reason the church grew.

In addition to providing for the members of a particular assembly, congregations of the New Testament church gave money to other congregations in distress. This concern is most evident in the money that churches throughout the Roman Empire collected and sent with Paul and Barnabas for the church in Jerusalem.[7] Powell reminds us that Paul strongly disagreed with James, who led the church of Jerusalem. In Galatians, Paul refers to James as an "acknowledged" leader and pillar, implying that James was not a true leader and pillar, and suggesting it was James who had sent the people responsible for creating conflict in Paul's congregation in Antioch. For Powell, the fact that Paul traveled the world collecting money for a church led by someone with whom he had divisive political and theological disagreements attests to what an important priority providing for churches in need was for the New Testament church.[8]

Of course, the New Testament church was also concerned with financing evangelism—sharing the good news of Jesus with the world. Just as generous women financed Jesus's own ministry, generous givers provided for the church's mission of bringing the gospel to the world (Luke 8:1–3). From the very beginning, this mission included caring for the poor and attending to people's physical as well as spiritual needs. This is evident in Matthew's Gospel. While Jesus's Great Commission is to make disciples, baptize, and teach, when Jesus comes in glory, he will judge according to whether we fed the hungry, gave the thirsty something to drink, clothed the naked, welcomed strangers, and visited those in prison (Matt. 25:31–46; 28:18–20).

An Act of Resistance

Closely related to participating in God's reign, we give as *an act of resistance* to the powers at work in the world that are opposed to God. Timothy V. Olson, lead pastor for mission and vision of Holy Trinity Lutheran Church in Ankeny, Iowa, names one of those powers as our "culture of affluence."[9] Charles Campbell, who teaches preaching at Duke Divinity School, calls this power "Mammon." Both agree that mammon and affluence are *powers* at work in our lives and in the world, as Legion was in the Gospels (Mark 5:9–13; Luke 8:30). Campbell writes, "In American culture, no greater power holds spirits captive than Mammon."[10] In this culture, where some people are affluent, the power of wealth, affluence, or mammon drives everyone to so desire affluence that we place value on and take pride in the possession of material things and inflict shame on those who lack possessions. By both obvious and insidious means, affluence or mammon drives everyone, including those with everything and those with nothing, to desire and acquire more and to do whatever it takes to keep what they have. In this culture, Jesus's words ring especially true: "No slave can serve two masters; for a slave will either hate the one and love the other, or be devoted to the one and despise the other. You cannot serve God and wealth" (Luke 16:13).

Campbell argues that in a culture where spirits are shaped by accumulation and mammon promises security, giving money away is an act of resistance to the power of mammon, which seeks to enslave us. Campbell rightly observes that giving away money is one of the faith practices by which Christians "publicly embody their loyalty to the living God, rather than to the lesser powers that seek to become idols."[11] Giving money away is a concrete means of living into the new life accomplished in Jesus's life, death, and resurrection. We do not overcome the "power" of money by accumulating more money, by using money for good purposes, or by being just and fair in our financial dealings. These are still ways we participate in buying and selling. We participate in God's work of liberation, reconciliation, and recreation when we give money away, rendering money powerless and freeing ourselves—and all people—from its oppressive control. Campbell observes that when Christians resist the power of mammon by giving away money, money becomes a sign of grace rather than domination. Jesus named us "light of the world" and "salt of the earth" (Matt. 5:13–16). Resisting the powers by giving money away is one way that we are.

Describing stewardship as an act of resistance invites the church to transform giving from a routine matter into a discipline by which believers resist the powers of death at work in the world. Campbell warns that this might be dangerous to the institutional church, if members begin to question whether the way the church uses its own money, particularly its accumulation of endowments, is a sign of its own captivity to the power of mammon. As daring as it is to give money away in a culture of accumulation, Christians and the church can be even more audacious by giving money away secretly, so that the left hand does not know what the right hand is doing (Matt. 6:3). Not knowing who else to thank, those who benefit from the money Christians and the church give away can only thank God.

While I did not initially name giving money away an act of resistance to the powers of death at work in the world, I came to understand Jesus's teaching about that demanding power wealth holds over us when I finally *heard* Jesus's parable of the rich fool (Luke 12:13–21), which I have come to know as the parable of the barns. I always heard God saying to the rich man, "This very night, I am demanding your life of you." But this is not what God says. In this parable, God says to the rich man, "This very night your life is being demanded of you. And the things you have prepared, whose will they be?" (Luke 12:20). In a sermon entitled "The Demands of Our Barns," which is printed below, I wonder whether the things the rich man prepared—his barns—are demanding his life.[12]

THE DEMANDS OF OUR BARNS

As I get older, Jesus's parable of the rich fool (Luke 12:13–21) gets harder and harder to deal with. We all know the story.

> The land of a rich man produced abundantly. And this man thought to himself, "What shall I do, for I have no place to store my crops?" Then he said, "I will do this: I will pull down my barns, and build larger ones, and there I will store all my grain and my goods. And I will say to my soul, Soul, you have ample goods laid up for many years; relax, eat, drink, be merry." But God said to him, "You fool! This very night your life is being demanded of you. And the things you have prepared, whose will they be?"

When I was younger, I found it easy to rail against being overly concerned with filling our barns and storing up treasure for tomorrow rather than being rich toward God. As I saw it, there was plenty of time to plan for the future. It seems that I was not alone in my thinking. I heard on the news recently that 53 percent of Americans have less than a thousand dollars in savings. Economists wish that we would put a little more energy into filling up our barns. In all honesty, we are worse off than the rich man in Jesus's parable. He was storing for the future, saving for a rainy day, providing for his old age. Our greed is different. We want to "relax, eat, drink, and be merry" now, despite the fact that we don't "have ample goods laid up for many years." Rather than hoarding for the future, we have to have it all right now—the best, the biggest, the fastest, and the most.

This summer, my family and I spent a week on a charming inland lake in Michigan, where we've vacationed for the past few years. This year things were different. Cottages were being torn down and replaced with castles. Building larger houses is our society's equivalent of building bigger barns. My wife and I wondered how people could afford it. Then we learned that our nation's credit card debt is soaring. Some reports say that the average American carries $70,000 in credit card debt. And we are passing this greed on to our children, who just can't understand why they can't have it all, right now. Not only don't many kids today understand the meaning of the word "no," they've never even heard the word. Case in point is the twelve-year-old, interviewed on MSNBC, who was totally dejected because her dad wouldn't pay for the cell phone that she needs. And this young person isn't alone. We all *need* so much in order to live!

Yes, Jesus's parable gives us pause, but not in the way that Jesus might expect. Our greed is not about hoarding for tomorrow; it's about having it all today. But those words from God still cause us to swallow hard, at least for a moment. "You fool! This very night your life is being demanded of you. And the things you have prepared, whose will they be?" We all know people who have had their life demanded of them. We can all name people who found themselves in situations where tragedy strikes and all that they have amounts to nothing: the freak accident, the terminal or debilitating illness, the fracture of the family, the loss of a child, the attack of addiction or abuse, the victimization of crime, sudden and unexpected death. "You fool! This very night your life is being demanded of you. And the things you have prepared, whose will they be?" Yes, these words from on high bring us up short and cause us to pause. But we soon realize that it's demoralizing to live as though we're going to die "this very night." We have to take our chances. And so we get over Jesus's parable. We get back to business as usual.

But what if Jesus is pointing out something more sinister, something more inevitable? What if, rather than pointing out something that *might* happen, Jesus is pointing out something that *will* happen? What if it wasn't God demanding the rich man's life? If we look at Luke 12:20 a second time, we will notice that God does not say, "This very night I demand your life of you." God says, "This very night your life is being demanded of you." What if, instead of God, the rich man's barns are demanding his life?

How can the rich man's barns demand his life? Whether we're hoarding for tomorrow or striving to have it all today, filling, maintaining, and protecting our barns is demanding work. If we're not on our guard against all kinds of greed, the abundance of possessions can end up demanding our whole life. The big house never really becomes a home because we're never there; we're always at work. Our kids have everything, except us at our best and time just to be together as a family. In our most significant relationships, we get so caught up in keeping up that we lose track of intimacy and the delight in one another that brought us together. Friendships get lost in the fast pace of life; we're just too busy. Our relationship to our work changes; no longer a calling or a vocation, it becomes a way to make money. Over time, we no longer know, let alone like, who we are. Our life is lost to the demands of our barns. But, hey, want to see my new _____? You fill in the blank.

Jesus's parable and God's pronouncement are not a judgment but a warning. "Take care!" Jesus says, "Be on your guard against all kinds of greed; for one's life does not consist in the abundance of possessions" (Luke 12:15). "You fool! This very night your life is being demanded of you. And the things you have prepared, whose will they be?" (Luke 12:20). Jesus is warning us against the dangers, the dire consequences, of trusting our security to our possessions, to what is created, and not to our Creator. When we attempt to find life by enslaving ourselves to our possessions, we wind up dead, not because God turns God's back on us, but because we empty ourselves of all the real life that God gives. On the cross Jesus gave the world real life. In the resurrection Jesus made that life eternal. In baptism Jesus gave this new and eternal life *to us*.

The challenge here is not to abandon our barns or to give away our goods. It's harder than that. The challenge here is to trust our security—our future and the quality of our life today—to the life that God in Christ gives and not to our stock portfolios, our Roth IRAs, and all the stuff that we *need* to live. We need to plan for tomorrow, yes. We also need to have faith for tomorrow.

This parable is penetrating and pointed. The older we get, the harder this parable gets, because we do worry about the future. Jesus reminds us that we cannot secure our future by building bigger barns and storing for ourselves. Our barns will end up demanding our life and leaving us empty. Real life and true security are ours in Christ. In Christ, we do not need to be independent and self-sufficient. More than God's creatures, we are God's children. When we get so caught up in building a life for ourselves that we lose track of what it means to live, God will have something to say about our present as surely as God has a hand in determining our future. The question is, will we receive God's involvement as an abrasive interruption of our plans, as the rich man did in Jesus's parable, or will we invite God in with trust and openness?

Bearing Witness

Giving as a way of resisting the power of mammon has a positive side. Giving is also a way we *bear witness to God as giver and provider, and ourselves as stewards or caretakers* of everything that God gives to us. "What do you have that you did not receive?" Paul asks. "And if you received it, why do you boast as if it were not a gift?" (1 Cor. 4:7). Scripture reminds us that everything we have and everything we are is a gift from God. Because God created us, nothing is our own—not our time, property, influence, faculties, bodies, or spirits. From a Christian perspective, this is doubly true, because God not only created us. Paul reminds us that we are not our own because Christ bought us with a price (1 Cor. 6:19, 20).

Because everything we have comes from God, and because we belong to God, we trust God to care for us and provide us with everything we need to be content. Jesus says of food and drink and clothing, "For it is the nations of the world that strive after all these things, and your Father knows that you need them" (Luke 12:30). Trusting God, we strive to follow Paul's instructions: "Do not worry about anything, but in everything by prayer and supplication with thanksgiving let your requests be made known to God. . . . And my God will fully satisfy every need of yours according to his riches in glory in Christ Jesus" (Phil. 4:6, 19).

We all know that what we do with our money reveals our priorities, our commitments, and our values. We bear witness to God as giver and provider when we put our faith in action by giving. Giving as bearing witness to God is not so much *giving away* as *giving back* to the One from whom we received, God who owns everything. Giving back as a witness to God our giver and provider is most striking in the Acts of the Apostles. We have seen how, when people became Christian, they renounced the ownership of all their possessions and of themselves and gave everything back to God through the church (Acts 2:42–45; 4:32–35).

While we bear witness to God as the owner of everything, we also acknowledge our identity as stewards rather than owners. In the Bible, a *steward* is the person the master entrusts with the responsibility of caring for and watching over the household. A steward is a guardian or trustee. God chose humanity to be God's stewards, to have dominion over all that God has made and to care for God's creation. "God blessed them, and God said to them, 'Be fruitful and multiply, and fill the earth and subdue it; and have dominion over the fish of the sea and over the birds of the air and over every living thing that moves upon the earth'" (Gen. 1:28). God further entrusted Christians with the gift of the gospel. Paul writes, "All this is from God, who reconciled us to himself through Christ, and has given us the ministry of reconciliation; that is, in Christ God was reconciling the world to himself, not counting their trespasses against them, and entrusting the message of reconciliation to us. So we are ambassadors for Christ, since God is making his appeal through us; we entreat you on behalf of Christ, be reconciled to God" (2 Cor. 5:18–20). Powell contends that the good news in understanding ourselves as stewards is the freedom that comes from knowing who the owner is.[13] God owns everything; we do not.

Preaching on the blessings and woes in Jesus's Sermon on the Plain (Luke 6:20–32), Seth Moland-Kovash, copastor of All Saints Lutheran Church in Palatine, Illinois, names the congregation as both rich and poor and empowers them to share as a witness to the gospel. I entitled his sermon "The End of God's Story for You Is Blessing."[14]

THE END OF GOD'S STORY FOR YOU IS BLESSING

John is hungry. Sometimes John knows that hunger in spiritual and emotional ways. John is hungry for a place of belonging. John is hungry to know that his life matters. John is hungry to experience a deep and real relationship. John is hungry to love and to be loved. Those spiritual and emotional hungers are deep and profound and affect his life in lots of ways that he's aware of . . . and even more ways that he's not aware of. John's spiritual hunger sometimes makes his life unbearable.

But the spiritual hunger isn't the end of John's story. You see, John is also hungry. By which I mean, hungry. John is hungry for love and affection and meaning and purpose. And John is hungry for bread. John doesn't have enough to make ends meet. John's never sure whether to pay his rent or his medical bills or his court fees or to buy groceries. He's never sure there will be enough to get it all done. He's never sure whether the hunger in his belly will be filled.

And Jesus said, "Blessed are you who are poor, for yours is the kingdom of God. Blessed are you who are hungry now, for you will be filled."

Jane is rich, frankly. Jane has a beautiful home (well, homes). Jane has fulfilled all of her dreams in her career. She is able to go on vacation a few times a year, she can indulge every once in a while in that really good bottle of wine or buy herself a really expensive pair of shoes. She's worked hard, and she's been blessed because of it. She shares generously. She gives to her church and to lots of other agencies that help people who are less fortunate. People like John. Jane has more than enough that she can share.

And Jesus said, "Woe to you who are rich, for you have received your consolation. Woe to you who are full now, for you will be hungry."

Now I'm assuming that each of you are sitting there trying to identify with either John or Jane. You're trying to see whether you're one of the haves or one of the have-nots. You're trying to see whether you're hungry or whether you're full now. And because of the way that Jesus promises things will be turned upside down, we all actually want to identify ourselves with John. We want to be promised God's blessing and not God's woe.

But the truth is that life is not nearly that black and white. Life is not nearly that neat and clean. None of us is John the hungry one or Jane the rich one. All of us, all of us saints here at All Saints, are John the hungry one *and* Jane the rich one—and not just from one day to the next or one year to the next, but all at the same time.

We are the rich. On any global scale we are all exceedingly and ridiculously wealthy. We are the rich ones who still struggle to make mortgage payments or who lose our jobs and the security and meaning and purpose involved in that.

We are the ones who are full now. We have enough to eat. We are the full ones who still find ourselves hungry for community and for meaning and for purpose—and for good things to eat.

We are the ones who are laughing now. We have entertainment and fellowship and laughter at our fingertips. We are the ones whose laughing turns to weeping in broken relationships, in pain and in mourning for suffering and dying friends and neighbors and family members.

We are John and Jane. We are laughing and weeping, full and hungry, rich and poor. All of us.

And into our laughing, crying, full, hungry, messy lives steps Jesus. In steps Jesus with a word of hope and promise. In steps Jesus with a word of blessing. In steps Jesus with the encouragement to live our lives in hope, because God's tomorrow is better than today.

You see, God has a blessing in store for you and for the whole world. Blessing is the end of God's story for you. Hunger is not the end of God's story for you. A lack of resources is not the end of God's story for you. Hopelessness is not the end of God's story for you. Spiritual hunger and physical hunger are not the end of God's story for you. Limits are not the end of God's story for you. Sickness and disease are not the end of God's story for you. Weeping and mourning are not the end of God's story for you. Death is not the end of God's story for you. Not having enough is not the end of God's story for you.

The end of God's story is always blessing. The end of God's story is always life. The end of God's story is always hope. The end of God's story is always enough. The end of God's story is always more than enough. God's story for you always ends in hope and wholeness. And life. Life is the end of God's story for you. Blessing is the end of God's story for you. God's tomorrow is always more hopeful than today. As people of faith, we walk knowing that our path ends in light.

It may be difficult now. There may be unbalanced budgets now. There may be shortages now. There may be tough sacrifices made now. There may be hospital visits and painful conversations with surgeons now. But God's tomorrow is hope. God's tomorrow is blessing. We walk into that blessing together. We walk into that hope together. We remind one another of the blessings. We embody the blessings for one another. And we claim the blessings together.

Whenever you share the blessings you've been given. Whenever you share your time, your talent, or your treasure. Whenever you share whatever blessings God has particularly given to you—whether it's here at All Saints or in your workplace or school or neighborhood—whenever you share blessings, you are bearing witness. You're bearing witness that God has hope in store for the world, that God has blessing in store for the world, that God has life in store for the world. Blessed are you. And blessed is the world through you. Amen.

Growing in Grace

As we give to worship God, resist the powers, and bear witness to others, we also benefit ourselves. "But grow in the grace and knowledge of our Lord and Savior Jesus Christ" (2 Pet. 3:18). Timothy V. Olson suggested to me that giving, specifically tithing, is a biblical and spiritual discipline by which *God enters into our lives and shapes us* in a way that our imagination, our thoughts, and our words cannot. Through the discipline of giving, God graciously invites us both to gratefully respond to God for blessings received and to faithfully follow a path toward freedom from the economic powers that bind us.[15] The spiritual discipline of giving—like worship, prayer, fasting, reading Scripture, and works of charity—is a way that we live out the salvation we received from Christ and not a means of earning salvation from Christ. Like all spiritual disciplines, giving is a way we invite or ask God to continue to shape us into the image of Christ by engaging in a practice that brings us further into the kingdom of God. Pastor Olson observes that we do not engage the discipline of giving "reluctantly or under compulsion, for God loves a cheerful giver" (2 Cor. 9:7).

Disciplines of any kind help us to deal with the duality of our human nature as saint and sinner. "For where your treasure is, there your heart will be also," Jesus says, and, "No one can serve two masters; for a slave will either hate the one and love the other, or be devoted to the one and despise the other. You cannot serve God and wealth" (Matt. 6:21, 24). We give as a spiritual discipline so that we use material possessions, money, and the things that money can buy, rather than serving them. While we may be keenly aware that what we do with our money reveals our priorities, our values, or our "heart," giving as a spiritual discipline has a different effect. The way we spend our money, where we put our treasure, will shape, even determine, the people we become. So, when we place our treasure somewhere, whatever our treasure happens to be, our hearts will follow.[16] In this way, we become the people we want to be.

People who practice giving as one of their spiritual disciplines find themselves closer to God, spiritually blessed, and transformed from within. The good news of disciplining ourselves in this way is that "we can be free from that spiral of consumerism that allows financial concerns to rule our lives"[17] and become the people we most want to be.

Receiving

Some preachers teach that a reason for people to give is in part *to receive, to be blessed by God in the here and now.* In Matthew, for example, Jesus says, "But when you give alms, do not let your left hand know what your right hand is doing, so that your alms may be done in secret; and your Father who sees in secret will reward you" (Matt. 6:3–4). In Luke, Jesus appears to makes the reward more attractive: "Give, and it will be given to you. A good measure, pressed down, shaken together, running over, will be put into your lap; for the measure you give will be the measure you get back" (Luke 6:38). According to proponents of the "prosperity gospel"—or the gospel of health and wealth, as it is sometimes called—which became popular in the closing years of the twentieth century, God will not bless those who hold back even a portion from him. But those who give a tithe or more will be abundantly blessed in return by getting back all of the monetary investment and more. According to Paul, "The point is this: the one who sows sparingly will also reap sparingly, and the one who sows bountifully will also reap bountifully. . . . You will be enriched in every way for your great generosity" (2 Cor. 9:6, 11). The prosperity gospel fits well with our notions that "everything happens for a reason" and "every dog gets his day." God rewards us for giving up material things with a superabundance of material things.

Yet, while we can point to a few passages that seem to suggest we give in order to receive material prosperity, recognition, or power and influence, the bulk of Scripture indicates that God does not work this way. God gives first, and God gives without regard for what we do or do not give. For example, Powell points out that the prophet Amos reminded Israel they received God's most abundant blessing when they were physically and spiritually wandering in the wilderness, and not when they were willing and able to offer their tithes (Amos 4:4; 5:25).[18] Paul proclaims, "God proves his love for us in that while we still were sinners Christ died for us" (Rom. 5:8). The writer of 1 Timothy decries the desire for material wealth, warning, "Those who want to be rich fall into temptation and are trapped by many senseless and harmful desires that plunge people into ruin and destruction. For the love of money is a root of all kinds of evil, and in their eagerness to be rich some have wandered away from the faith and pierced themselves with many pains" (6:9–10).

What are we to make of passages that indicate God blesses or rewards faithfulness in matters of financial stewardship? It is essential to distinguish between material and spiritual rewards. For example, Jesus declares, "And everyone who has left houses or brothers or sisters or father or mother or children or fields, for my name's sake, will receive a hundredfold, and will inherit eternal life" (Matt. 19:29). The fate of the apostles—various forms of homicide or martyrdom—makes plain that the "hundredfold" they received was not quantified in houses, families, and fields. Rather, they and we receive the peace, joy, and satisfaction of participating in the reign of God. Jesus affirms this understanding when he says, "And you will be blessed, because they cannot repay you, for you will be repaid at the resurrection of the righteous" (Luke 14:14). Yet, more important than the nature of God's reward is the nature of our giving. Powell asserts, "God rewards *unselfish* faithfulness, good deeds that are performed for their own sake rather than simply as crass attempts at earning a reward."[19] Jesus says, "But love your enemies, do good, and lend, expecting nothing in return. Your reward will be great, and you will be children of the Most High; for he is kind to the ungrateful and the wicked" (Luke 6:35).

As some people might give to receive material prosperity, others might give to receive the church's recognition and the power and influence that comes with an elevated status within the faith community. That people give to be recognized is nothing new. Jesus describes people who sound a trumpet in the synagogues and in the streets when they give alms so that people might praise them (Matt. 6:2). Today the church puts up plaques and names fellowship halls and endowed chairs to recognize and honor generous givers. Church fund-raisers point out that Jesus publicly recognized the extravagant giving of the widow, and Paul boasted about the overwhelming generosity of the Macedonian churches (Mark 12:41–44; 2 Cor. 8:1–6). Jesus calls those who give to be recognized "hypocrites" and declares, "Truly I tell you, they have received their reward" (Matt. 6:2). Though Jesus and Paul recognized generosity, neither the widow nor the Macedonian churches gave to be recognized by others. Jesus says to the part of us desiring recognition,

"So you also, when you have done all that you were ordered to do, say, 'We are worthless slaves; we have done only what we ought to have done!'" (Luke 17:10).

Finally, we have all experienced people who give to receive power and influence within the church. I suspect that we can all name times when we have accorded generous givers an added measure of influence or yielded to their desires in matters that we conclude really do not matter anyway. We may even know or be a pastor or a congregational member who attempts to wield power and influence based on the money the congregation contributes to (or can withhold from) the diocese or denomination, a cause or an agency. The Epistle of James suggests that such "acts of favoritism" indicate that a congregation does not really believe in Jesus Christ. According to James, when a Christian assembly favors or privileges the rich over the poor, they make distinctions and become judges with evil thoughts. "Listen, my beloved brothers and sisters," James exhorts. "Has not God chosen the poor in the world to be rich in faith and to be heirs of the kingdom that he has promised to those who love him?" (James 2:1–5). Jesus says to those who seek power and influence within the Christian community, "The greatest among you must become like the youngest, and the leader like one who serves" (Luke 22:26). What advice would the "greatest among us"—the youngest and those who serve—offer about how we use our money?

Whether we give as an act of worship or an act of resistance, to participate in or bear witness to the gospel, or to grow in grace or receive God's blessings, we give in response to the gospel—the love and life God gives us in Jesus Christ. Giving in response to the gospel shapes how we give and the attitude with which we give. In the next chapter, I explore what the Bible has to say about the spirit of our giving.

AS YOU PREPARE YOUR SERMON . . .

- What Bible story or verse would you use to answer the question of why you give to God or the church? Does this story or verse connect with any of the biblical reasons for giving presented in this chapter? If so, which one(s)?

- How concerned are the members of your congregation with what becomes of the money they give? What does this say about their reason for giving?

- How does your congregation's budget reflect the New Testament church's financial priorities of providing for the poor, supporting other congregations, and spreading the gospel?

- Name one way that mammon or affluence exerts power in your life and in the life of your congregation. Name one way you and your congregation can give money away as an act of resistance. Name one way you and your congregation can give money away to bear witness to the gospel.

- How might your congregation invite, encourage, and support giving as a spiritual discipline? What "word picture" of giving as a spiritual discipline might be included in a sermon?

- In a culture marked by consumerism and entitlement, how do we faithfully preach about receiving blessings from giving?

- What advice would the "greatest among us"—the youngest and those who serve—offer about how we use our money? Who might you ask to find out?

CHAPTER 5

How Does the Bible Say We Are to Give?

EVERY NOW AND AGAIN, I amuse myself by imagining preaching a stewardship sermon that lifts up Ananias and his wife Sapphira as biblical models of giving (Acts 4:32—5:11). Acts reports that everyone in the nascent Christian community—including "a Levite, a native of Cyprus, Joseph, to whom the apostles gave the name Barnabas (which means 'son of encouragement')" (4:36)—sold the lands and houses they owned and laid the proceeds at the apostles' feet, and the money was distributed so "there was not a needy person among them" (4:34). Everyone in the Christian community did this except Ananias and Sapphira.

Ananias sold his field and, "with his wife's knowledge, he kept back some of the proceeds, and brought only a part and laid it at the apostles' feet" (5:2). Peter called Ananias out on this publicly, asking Ananias why Satan filled his heart to lie to the Holy Spirit and to keep back part of the proceeds of the land. Of course, to make this fantasy sermon work, we need to abandon a careful reading of the text, because Peter distinguishes between withholding some of the proceeds, which is permissible, and lying about it to God, which is not. Downplaying or skipping over this distinction, we move on to the fact that, when Ananias heard Peter's words, "he fell down and died. And great fear seized all who heard of it" (5:5).

The story does not stop here. After young men carried Ananias's body out and buried him, Sapphira came in unaware of what had happened. When Peter asked her whether she and her husband had given all the proceeds from the sale of their field to the church and she indicated that they had, Sapphira immediately fell down at Peter's feet and died. "And great fear seized the whole church and all who heard of these things" (5:11). In my fantasy stewardship sermon, I would retell this episode from Acts like a ghost story. Then, with scriptural warrant, I would instill the fear of God in the hearts of the faithful and proclaim, "Give or die!" Since I am an accomplished preacher, people would give, at least for the next few weeks until their fear subsided. I call this a fantasy sermon because I would never preach it—and neither should you!

Sermons that seek to motivate people to give out of fear are not as far-fetched as we sometimes assume. I shared in chapter 2 that for fifty years beginning in the 1870s, Christian stewardship literature was filled with the notion that the failure to give at least a tithe or 10 percent to the church was tantamount to robbing God. As these preachers interpreted Malachi 3:8–10, God will curse those who rob God. In chapter 2, I shared this approach to stewardship in order to argue theologically that the way preachers ask people to give must be consistent with the gospel and so should not leave people feeling manipulated, coerced, or afraid. As the author of 1 John says, "There is no fear in love, but perfect love casts out fear; for fear has to do with punishment, and whoever fears has not reached perfection in love. We love because he first loved us" (1 John 4:18, 19). Yet, content is not the only aspect of a sermon that can be inconsistent with the gospel. The gospel can be invalidated by the way a sermon is delivered.

Assuming a preacher is proclaiming the gospel, that message is undermined and even negated when a sermon's tone contradicts the sermon's message. I say this for more than theological reasons. Preaching with a tone that is congruent with the message is essential for effective communication. Tone is especially important in overcoming the knowledge, attitude, feelings, and prior experience the listeners bring, which may inhibit or prevent their receiving and responding positively to the message. When preaching aims at getting people to change their attitudes and behavior, the tone of sermons is ordinarily positive, hopeful, and encouraging so that it inspires and encourages. The tone of the sermon must also be authentic. Congregations can tell when preachers force or attempt to fake an attitude. In those situations, the congregation takes home the message that the preacher communicates nonverbally and in the tone of her or his voice rather than whatever the preacher happens to be saying. Preachers therefore cultivate in themselves the attitude of spirit they wish to impart to their hearers.

In sermons about money and giving, the tone of our preaching needs to be consistent with and cultivate the spirit of giving that we wish to instill in our people. If we preach fear, people will feel afraid and give out of fear, which is inconsistent with giving in response to the gospel. Scripture teaches us to give (1) gratefully, (2) freely, (3) cheerfully, (4) generously, (5) obediently, and (6) intentionally. Therefore, preachers should use these attitudes as the tone or spirit of stewardship sermons. While it is certainly possible to combine these attitudes and, for example, invite people to give cheerfully and obediently or freely and generously, a single, prevalent attitude in a particular sermon works best. Cultivating these attitudes when preaching about money further ensures that people are asked to give in response to the gospel.

In this chapter, I reflect on these biblical attitudes toward giving and suggest ways of creating them in the stewardship sermon. Whatever tone preachers choose, we need to remain vigilant in preaching that this attitude toward God transcends giving to the church. When the church instills freedom, gratitude, joy, generosity, and obedience in its members only toward the church, the church is not faithful to the gospel. Our goal is that people of faith live from these attitudes toward God in all aspects of life.

Give Gratefully

The psalmist declares, "What shall I return to the Lord for all his bounty to me?" (Ps. 116:12). I learned this verse with the words *render* and *benefits* by singing them in worship every Sunday as the ushers brought our gifts of money, bread, and wine to the altar. "What shall I render to the Lord for all his benefits to me?" As our congregation sang it, the psalm continued, "I will offer the sacrifice of thanksgiving, and will call on the name of the Lord."[1] The melody was joyful and uplifting, and if you had asked us in that moment, "Why do you give to the church?" the likely response would be, "Out of gratitude for all God has done for us!"

Asking people to give gratefully is possible only when they are genuinely thankful for what has been done for them and given to them without price. Preaching that appeals to gratitude therefore needs to do more than tell people that they should feel grateful. Preaching needs to make people feel grateful and leave people feeling grateful. One way to do this is to gratefully and concretely recount everything that God has done for us. I often think of the seder or Passover song "Dayenu," which approximately means "It would have been enough. . . ." The song has fifteen stanzas describing what God has done for the Jewish people—five about freedom from slavery, five about miracles or signs, and five about a close relationship with God. The recurring theme is "It would have been enough, but God did so much more!" A stewardship sermon might be crafted as its own form of "Dayenu":

> God created us together with all that exists, and God provides us with all that we have—food and clothing, home and family, reason and abilities, comfort and protection. And it would have been enough. But "God proves his love for us in that while we still were sinners Christ died for us" (Rom. 5:8). And it would have been enough. But God receives our prayers. God bears our burdens. God shares in our rejoicing. And it would have been enough. But by the power of the Holy Spirit, God governs and guides our lives so that we manage our affairs more faithfully than we would on our own. And it would have been enough.

The preacher might then name blessings that the community, congregation, and individuals within the faith community received from God, including the refrain, "And it would have been enough." The sermon would then move to naming our gratitude and inviting the congregation to give or respond.

Alternatively, the preacher might use biblical images to invite the members of the congregation to recall a time when they were particularly grateful to God. For example, perhaps someone can relate to the woman caught in adultery, to whom Jesus said, "Woman, where are they? Has no one condemned you? . . . Neither do I condemn you. Go your way, and from now on do not sin again" (John 8:10–11). Perhaps someone identifies with the tenth leper, who, "when he saw that he was healed, turned back, praising God with a loud voice. He prostrated himself at Jesus's feet and thanked him. And he was a Samaritan" (Luke 17:15–16). Perhaps someone is grateful for the company and support of believers, as Paul was. Luke reports, "The believers from [Rome], when they heard of us, came as far as the Forum of Appius and Three Taverns to meet us. On seeing them, Paul thanked God and took courage" (Acts 28:15). Personally, I am a fan of the widow of Zarephath, who along with her household ate for many days by God's grace. "The jar of meal was not emptied, neither did the jug of oil fail, according to the word of the Lord that he spoke by Elijah" (1 Kings 17:16). The preacher might speak to the entire congregation and remember aloud moments when God blessed his people in this place with "the good wine" (John 2:10) or "many wonders and signs" (Acts 2:43).

The danger of this approach to preaching, of course, is some people in the assembly have not experienced these blessings. Rather than the support of the Christian community, some are subjected to the church's condemnation, abandonment, and betrayal. We all pray for people who grow sicker instead of being healed. Rather than eating for many days, some in our congregations do not have enough for today. Some congregations choke on inferior wine in more ways than drinking what is served at the communion table and cannot recall the last time they witnessed signs and wonders. Still, this is the risk preachers and congregations take whenever we break open God's Word. Jesus himself indicated that not everyone receives the blessings they long for or, Jesus's hearers might argue, they deserve: "But the truth is, there were many widows in Israel in the time of Elijah, when the heaven was shut up three years and six months, and there was a severe famine over all the land; yet Elijah was sent to none of them except to a widow at Zarephath in Sidon. There were also many lepers in Israel in the time of the prophet Elisha, and none of them was cleansed except Naaman the Syrian" (Luke 4:25–28). Confronted by this reality, I readily identify with all in the synagogue at Nazareth who were filled with rage. Perhaps you do as well. Yet, the fact that God's blessings are not true for everyone in the same way does not make them untrue.

Rather than avoiding naming God's blessings, preachers need to assure their hearers that the absence of blessings is not an indication that God does not love us, has abandoned us, or is punishing us. Upon hearing of Galileans whose blood Pilate mingled with their sacrifices, Jesus asks, "Do you think that because these Galileans suffered in this way they were worse sinners than all other Galileans? . . . Or those eighteen who were killed when the tower of Siloam fell on them—do you think that they were worse offenders than all the others living in Jerusalem?" (Luke 13:2–4). Jesus's answer is a resounding "No!" Sometimes, suffering is a consequence of our actions. It is always an indication of our imperfect lives and our fallen world. Suffering is never God's will or God's work.

At this point in the sermon, the preacher might remind the congregation that our gratitude to God transcends our circumstances because God always loves us, faithfully cares for us, and earnestly desires the best for us. Jesus explains to Nicodemus, "Indeed, God did not send the Son into the world to condemn the world, but in order that the world might be saved through him" (John 3:17). Contrasting himself with a thief, our good shepherd declares, "The thief comes only to steal and kill and destroy. I came that they may have life, and have it abundantly" (John 10:10). The good news is that we can be grateful in every circumstance because God has been and is faithful to us. As Paul writes, "I have learned to be content with whatever I have. I know what it is to have little, and I know what it is to have plenty. In any and all circumstances I have learned the secret of being well-fed and of going hungry, of having plenty and of being in need. I can do all things through him who strengthens me" (Phil. 4:11–13).

The key to giving to God gratefully is receiving from God gratefully. When we give to God out of gratitude, God is pleased. Speaking through the psalmist, the LORD God declares, "Those who bring thanksgiving as their sacrifice honor me" (Ps. 50:23).

Give Freely

Paul testifies that the churches of Macedonia "voluntarily gave according to their means, and even beyond their means, begging us earnestly for the privilege of sharing in this ministry to the saints" (2 Cor. 8:3). Time and again, the church turned to Paul's testimony as verification that people should give freely rather than being or feeling compelled to give a certain amount. In chapter 1, I discussed the reasons why, despite its history of collecting money through various forms of tax, the church in North America determined that all church finance ought to be underwritten by freewill offerings, paid by rich and poor alike according to their ability. First, requiring people to pay for the church implied God's favor could be—or, worse, needed to be—bought, a position absolutely rejected by the Protestant Reformers. Second, even if requiring people to pay for the church was appropriate, the existence of more than one church in a community rendered such requirements impractical, because people could simply join a different church if they did not want to pay whatever fee was required.

At different times, required dues and taxes were not the only means of raising money apart from voluntary giving that the Protestant church in the United States rejected as inappropriate. For example, Jesus said, "Stop making my Father's house a marketplace!" (John 2:16). When I was growing up, our pastors taught that, with these words, Jesus disallowed holding bake sales, church bazaars, rummage sales, festivals, fish fries, raffles, and especially bingo in the church. The exception to this rule was the youth, who were assumed not to have money to freely give and to need to be taught the importance of earning their keep. Today, while the church's objection to fund-raising activities has lessened in many places, some church leaders worry that endowments negatively affect congregations by diminishing voluntary giving and making congregations less responsive to change and the needs of the surrounding community. For all sorts of reasons, churches continue to do their best to embrace Paul's testimony about voluntary giving and teach their members to join the psalmist in proclaiming, "With a freewill offering I will sacrifice to you" (Ps. 54:6). At the same time, many congregations struggle—or need to struggle—with the degree to which freewill offerings are supplemented by other "revenue streams," as well as the types of additional fund-raising that are (and are not) appropriate. These decisions will influence how one preaches giving freely.

Preachers obviously empower people to give freely by clearly giving them a choice. "Each of you must give as you have made up your mind," Paul writes, "not reluctantly or under compulsion" (2 Cor. 9:7). Preachers empower people to give freely when we make plain that our relationship with God and the church does not depend on what we put in the offering plate and do not even unintentionally hint or imply that it does. For example, preachers ought not say, "While your relationship with God in no way depends upon your pledge, if you take that relationship seriously, you will increase your pledge. As the Epistle of James says: 'For just as the body without the spirit is dead, so faith without works is also dead'" (2:26). This kind of message implies we do not really have a choice. Preachers truly free their congregations to give voluntarily by trusting that the proclamation of the gospel will get people to respond, and so we do not have to.

Give Cheerfully

"Each of you must give as you have made up your mind," Paul writes, "not reluctantly or under compulsion, for God loves a cheerful giver" (2 Cor. 9:7). Advocates of cheerful giving argue that when people give cheerfully, they are aware they are giving to God. Cheerful givers bring their gifts regularly to the church as an act of worship. They make their giving a subject of prayer. A cheerful gift represents a person's ability to financially participate in God's own mission and may even be a sacrifice. Giving cheerfully leads to spiritual growth.

Cheerful givers are less likely to give reluctantly or out of a sense of obligation or because they are afraid or out of a need for recognition. Cheerful givers are less concerned about whether their gifts are recognized or appreciated. While cheerful givers may care that what they give is put to the best possible use, this is not their motivation for giving, and so they are less likely to judge. Giving cheerfully is a concrete way to resist the power of recognition, appreciation, and judgment.

Giving cheerfully does not necessarily mean giving easily, painlessly, or comfortably. Christians give God thanks and praise for who God is at the same time they feel ashamed of themselves and what humanity has done to God's world. Christians remain hopeful even as they despair and remain faithful when they have every reason to doubt, so we can give cheerfully even when giving is not easy and may bring us discomfort. In this same spirit, Christians can give cheerfully even when giving is hard. In fact, some remarkable saints regularly give cheerfully as they grow in their giving or even give beyond their means. Mark Allan Powell suggests that these saints practice a degree of renunciation and self-denial in recognition of the spiritual principle, "Where your treasure is, there your heart will be also" (Matt. 6:21). Sacrificial giving undertaken cheerfully brings us closer to God and disciplines us to be the godly people we want to be.[2]

We are more likely to give cheerfully when we decide what to give for ourselves so that we also give freely. Preachers will therefore give their congregations a choice and encourage them to make a choice that brings joy. Preachers could then speak concretely about the joys of giving. Undertaken cheerfully, any of the reasons we give to God discussed in chapter 4—expressing love, making a difference, resisting evil, sharing our faith, and growing closer to Jesus—lead to joy. Of course, the truth that we give cheerfully because God has given us so much lies behind all of these reasons to give. The preacher should therefore give the congregation an experience of the gospel that leaves them feeling cheerful.

I sometimes think proclaiming the gospel is like serving someone a cup of coffee.[3] You cannot satisfy someone by describing a good cup of coffee, convince someone they had a good cup of coffee when the coffee they had was not good, or get people to respond to a bad cup of coffee the way they would respond to a good cup of coffee. Preaching the gospel works the same way. We cannot merely describe the gospel or convince people that whatever we preach instead of the gospel is the gospel or prescribe how they should respond to the gospel when we have not preached it. At its best, preaching does more than explain the gospel doctrinally or according to some formula. Preaching leaves people *tasting* the gospel. When people taste the gospel, they are hopeful, uplifted, and cheerful. They will respond cheerfully. If people do not taste the gospel, the rest really does not matter.

Give Generously

Turning again to Paul's testimony about the Macedonian churches, we see that giving generously is a sign that God is at work regardless of people's circumstances. Paul writes, "We want you to know, brothers and sisters, about the grace of God that has been granted to the churches of Macedonia; for during a severe ordeal of affliction, their abundant joy and their extreme poverty have overflowed in a wealth of generosity on their part. For, as I can testify, they voluntarily gave according to their means" (2 Cor. 8:1). From Paul's testimony, we can learn something very important about the nature of generosity.

Paul calls the Macedonians' generosity "the grace of God that has been granted to the churches." Powell understands generosity as one of the fruits of the Spirit. Powell points out that, according to Paul, "the fruit of the Spirit is love, joy, peace, patience, kindness, generosity, faithfulness, gentleness, and self-control" (Gal. 5:22, 23). As a fruit of the Holy Spirit, generosity is not something we conjure or cultivate all by ourselves. We become generous by "not quenching God's Spirit (1 Thessalonians 5:19), but allowing the transforming work of Christ to have its full effect in shaping us to be the people God wants us to be (Romans 12:2; 2 Corinthians 5:17; Galatians 2:20; Philippians 1:6)."[4]

Instead of telling their congregations to be generous, preachers might name the transforming power of Jesus to make them generous givers. Some consider Zacchaeus, the rich chief tax collector, as the prime example of Jesus's power to convert someone from greedy to generous. After Jesus called Zacchaeus down from his sycamore tree and informed Zacchaeus that he would be staying at his house, we read in the New Revised Standard Version of the Bible that Zacchaeus responded, "Look, half of my possessions, Lord, I will give to the poor; and if I have defrauded anyone of anything, I will pay back four times as much" (Luke 19:8). From this perspective, Jesus freed Zacchaeus from enslavement to the power of mammon.[5] New Testament scholar Walter E. Pilgrim writes, "The presence of Jesus makes possible what is humanly impossible. A wealthy man gets through the needle's eye! But not without some radical change."[6] In this portrait, Zacchaeus is akin to Ebenezer Scrooge. The drawback of this approach is that some people compare themselves to Scrooge, and Zacchaeus, and think to themselves, "I was never that bad—and could never be that good."

The New International Version translates Zacchaeus's words differently: "Look, Lord! Here and now I give half of my possessions to the poor, and if I have cheated anybody out of anything, I will pay back four times the amount." In the English Standard Version, we read that Zacchaeus says, "Behold, Lord, the half of my goods I give to the poor. And if I have defrauded anyone of anything, I restore it fourfold" (Luke 19:8). The future tense *will* is missing, implying Zacchaeus's conversion and radical change from greedy to generous are missing as well. Instead, Jesus frees and empowers Zacchaeus to confess his current generous practice—giving half his goods to the poor and *if* he defrauds anyone, restoring it fourfold. Joel B. Green, who teaches New Testament at Fuller Theological Seminary in Pasadena, California, observes, "Luke's narrative mentions nothing of Zacchaeus's need for repentance, act of repentance, or faith; nor of Jesus' summons to repentance; nor does he in any other way structure this episode as a 'story of conversion.' According to this reading, Zacchaeus does not resolve to undertake new practices but presents for Jesus' evaluation his current behaviors regarding money.[7] Read this way, Jesus's presence frees and empowers Zacchaeus to publicly name and claim his generosity rather than promise to make restitution for his sins. Professor Green continues, "Jesus' reference to 'salvation' (v. 9), then, signifies Zacchaeus's vindication and restoration to the community of God's people; he is not an outsider, after all, but has evidenced through his economic practices his kinship with Abraham (cf. 3:7–14)."[8] Presenting Zacchaeus as an example of someone committed to the values of Jesus's mission and describing Christ's transforming power in a way that is less instantaneous and extreme might open people who do not consider themselves in need of radical repentance, like the evil Zacchaeus preachers love to describe, to the possibility that Jesus can nevertheless move them toward greater generosity.

Alternatively, the preacher might inspire people to be more generous by helping them reframe their perspective on their lives, the church, and the world from scarcity to abundance. God created and provides a world characterized by abundance. Human beings err by assuming the world is marked by real scarcity and acting as if we do not or will not have enough. As Christians, our starting point is not what we lack but God's abundance and gracious giving of life, joy, salvation, and the material means of sustenance. A perspective of abundance is often the reason that congregants of modest means give with what others consider overwhelming generosity. Asked why they give so generously, these saints often respond, "Because God has richly blessed me."

Give Obediently

"All tithes from the land, whether the seed from the ground or the fruit from the tree, are the LORD's; they are holy to the LORD" (Lev. 27:30). For many Christians, giving is a matter of obeying God's command. In response to those who say that most giving in the New Testament was voluntary, advocates of biblical obligation assert that freewill offerings are gifts in addition to the fixed law of tithes and that the fixed law of tithes applies to all times, is obligatory under all circumstances, and prescribes the minimum standard for giving.

To make their case, advocates of biblical obligation attempt to show that New Testament texts about giving point back to the Old Testament. They then undertake to demonstrate that Christ and Paul endorsed the Law of Moses. They argue that, while Christ replaced the ceremonial rites and observances of the law, he did not nullify the moral law that

Moses represents. So, for example, in 1 Corinthians 9:7–14, advocates of biblical obligation understand that Paul is asserting Christ's plea for the financial support of his church and its ministers. They explain that when Paul asserts, "Who plants a vineyard and does not eat any of its fruit?" (v. 7), he is arguing that the church and its ministers are to receive one-tenth of people's income. For Paul "did not regard the law of Moses that provided for the maintenance of God's ministers as obsolete."[9]

According to Pat Robertson, founder of the Christian Broadcasting Network (CBN), the law of the tithe is not the only obligation at work; rather, there is also a law of reciprocity. "Christ's admonition to 'give and it will be given to you' defines a remarkable spiritual principle . . . [that] can also be called the law of reciprocity, which is quite evident in the physical world: for every action, there is an equal and opposite reaction. Smile at another person, and he'll probably smile back at you. Be critical of others, and they'll respond in kind. As you give, you will receive. Give generously, and you'll receive in like measure."[10] While God does not need our tithes, God instructs us to tithe so that we might learn the law of reciprocity. The CBN website then points to the reactions we can expect. Withholding the tithe is robbing God. Giving the tithe results in blessing. In my opinion, this transactional approach to giving runs contrary to the gospel.

Whether and how one preaches about giving obediently depends on how a given preacher and congregation understand biblical laws, such as the Ten Commandments. For example, the preacher and congregation might consider how they understand the ordination of women given the scriptural injunction that "women should be silent in the churches. For they are not permitted to speak, but should be subordinate, as the law also says" (1 Cor. 14:34). How does the congregation's teaching about divorce compare to Jesus's statement on divorce: "Anyone who divorces his wife and marries another commits adultery, and whoever marries a woman divorced from her husband commits adultery" (Luke 16:18). I am not advocating here for a particular understanding or use of the law. I am simply suggesting, as I did in chapter 3, that it is not credible for preachers to insist that laws related to giving constitute binding obligations and dismiss as no longer applicable biblical laws related to other areas of life.

Even advocates of biblical obligation do not want Christians to give only because God expects us to. They contend that sincerity in returning a portion of all God generously and abundantly gives is equally important. Giving only to receive blessings or avoid punishment is therefore inappropriate. The biblical commandment to tithe and the law of reciprocity are to be understood as standards to help Christians live according to God's will. We follow God's commandments out of love and respect. Some Christians find this paradox difficult to grasp. One congregant responded this way to a call to give obediently: "Just to make sure I understand, we give to God because we love him, right? But as I think about it, it kind of seems like there really isn't a choice."

Give Intentionally

"Each of you must give as you have made up your mind," Paul writes (2 Cor. 9:7). The church understands Paul's words to mean that Christians are to give intentionally, with forethought that has been bathed in prayer. Making up our minds does not mean deciding in the moment, as the offering plate passes before us. As Christians, we are to give according to a plan. Paul instructs the Corinthians, "On the first day of every week, each of you is to put aside and save whatever extra you earn, so that collections need not be taken when I come" (1 Cor. 16:2). Paul helps the Corinthians give intentionally by providing them with a plan.

Preachers might share the many spiritual benefits God gives us through intentional giving. An intentional giving plan helps us to remember God. As Moses exhorts Israel, "When the LORD your God has brought you into the land that he swore to your ancestors . . . and when you have eaten your fill, take care that you do not forget the LORD, who brought you out of the land of Egypt, out of the house of slavery" (Deut. 6:10–12). Setting aside our gifts, putting them in offering envelopes, and placing them in the offering plate provide a time and action by which we purposely remember God and God's will and work in the world. In this regard, some Christians experience intentional giving as prayer.

Intentional giving also brings us closer to and makes us more dependent upon God as we remain committed to our plan. During times when giving is difficult and we are tempted to keep everything for ourselves, giving intentionally keeps our lives from being ruled by our feelings and circumstances. Finally, the Holy Spirit works through a giving plan to transform us. As we give intentionally, the Holy Spirit increases in us the gift of generosity and shapes our priorities so our hearts will be where our treasure is. Moreover, the Holy Spirit helps us to do nothing from selfish ambition or conceit, to look not to our own interests but to the interests of others. In these ways, the Holy Spirit empowers us to let the same mind be in us that was in Christ Jesus, who emptied himself (Matt. 6:21; Luke 12:34; Phil. 2:3–7). In other words, as we give intentionally, the Holy Spirit brings us closer to becoming the people God would have us be.

Some faithful people genuinely resist planned giving because they experience determining what they will give well in advance of giving as undercutting what for them is the powerful experience of God preparing them to give on Sunday as they pray, study Scripture, and serve during the week. In truth, these saints are exercising their own plan for giving intentionally. Rather than attempting to correct or dissuade, the preacher does better to listen to and learn from these givers' experience and help them recognize they give according to a plan.

Church treasurers and finance committees tell us that giving intentionally also has financial benefits for the congregation. First, when members plan their giving and make those plans known to congregational leaders through pledging, the congregation can better plan its budget. Second, people who give intentionally generally give more, a little at a time, rather than giving somewhat larger gifts periodically, making it possible for the congregation to undertake more mission and ministry. "If every member increased their giving by this amount," church leaders sometimes argue, "we could . . ." Third, planned, regular giving helps the congregation manage cash flow.

Leaders who are more financially minded sometimes suggest that, while pastors and those more spiritually minded are moved to give by biblical and theological arguments, many others are motivated by what makes good financial sense. Congregations should certainly be aware of the financial benefits of planned giving. However, the pulpit is not the appropriate place for sharing this perspective, because, for example, congregational cash flow is not an appropriate sermon topic.

So what plan do we follow? Though Christians give freely in response to the gospel, we are helped and guided to give intentionally by looking to biblical models for giving. These standards include (1) giving regularly, (2) giving first fruits, (3) giving proportionately according to our means, (4) tithing, and (5) growing beyond the tithe. We choose to embrace and undertake one of these plans in response to God's grace. To help the faithful give intentionally, preachers and congregational leaders are responsible for teaching these biblical models. Exploring these models and reflecting on how much the Bible says we should give is the subject of chapter 6.

AS YOU PREPARE YOUR SERMON . . .

- How would you describe the general tone of the sermons that you preach and hear? What is the tone of sermons about money and giving? What taste do these sermons leave you with?

- Name a time when you and your congregation felt especially grateful to God. How might you keep this memory alive for yourself and your congregation?

- Who would you identify as a cheerful giver? What might that person want you to know about giving?

- What do you think of the idea that generosity is a gift of the Spirit? How might you cultivate this gift in your congregation?

- How are biblical commandments taught in your congregation? How will the way you understand the Law influence preaching about giving obediently?

CHAPTER 6

How Much Does the Bible Say We Should Give?

AS I RESEARCHED AND WROTE this book, I attempted to recall sermons I heard growing up that told or taught me how much to give to God or the church. I recall our pastor told us how we were to decide how much to give—prayerfully in response to the blessings we received. I do not recall our pastor ever telling us how much to give. Truthfully, I learned the most about giving to God when I was a child in Sunday school, through the songs we sang when the offering was collected. When I was very small, we sang "Hear the Pennies Dropping."

> HEAR THE PENNIES DROPPING,
> Listen while they fall.
> Ev'ry one for Jesus,
> He will get them all.
> *Refrain:*
>
> DROPPING, DROPPING, DROPPING, DROPPING,
> Hear the pennies fall;
> Ev'ry one for Jesus—
> He will get them all.
>
> DROPPING, DROPPING EVER,
> From each little hand.
> 'Tis our gift to Jesus,
> From his little band.
> *Refrain.*

Now, while we are little,
Pennies are our store,
But, when we are older,
Lord, we'll give thee more.
Refrain.

Though we have not money,
We can give him love;
He will own our off'ring,
Smiling from above.
Refrain.[1]

As we grew, the song changed to "We Give Thee But Thine Own."

We give Thee but Thine own,
Whate'er the gift may be;
All that we have is Thine alone,
A trust, O Lord, from Thee.

May we Thy bounties thus
As stewards true receive,
And gladly, as Thou blessest us,
To Thee our first fruits give.

Our hearts are bruised and dead,
And homes are bare and cold,
And lambs for whom the Shepherd bled
Are straying from the fold.

To comfort and to bless,
To find a balm for woe,
To tend the lone and fatherless
Is angels' work below.

The captive to release,
To God the lost to bring,
To teach the way of life and peace—
It is a Christ-like thing.

And we believe Thy Word,
Though dim our faith may be;
Whate'er for Thine we do, O Lord,
We do it unto Thee.[2]

While they do not cite chapter and verse, these Sunday school songs abound with biblical teachings about money and giving: we give in response to what God gives us; everything belongs to God or Jesus, who entrusts what we have to us; we are to give gladly, give our first fruits, and give in proportion to what we have; we give to participate in God's own work in the world; and we are to grow in our giving. These songs obviously omit any reference to how much we are to give. Unless, of course, we count "Ev'ry one for Jesus" and "All that we have is Thine alone, / A trust, O Lord, from Thee." These lyrics suggest the question that how much we give to God is inappropriate because everything belongs to God.

Give God Everything

According to Scripture, we begin to answer the question of how much we give to God by seriously acknowledging that, in actuality, we do not give anything to God because God owns everything. The psalmist declares, "The earth is the LORD's and all that is in it, the world, and those who live in it; for he has founded it on the seas, and established it on the rivers" (Ps. 24:1–2). God owns the world and all that is in it because God created it. Even though we might tell ourselves we earn our money by our own initiative, abilities, and hard work, Scripture reminds us that God provides the power, wisdom, and abilities with which we earn our living. In Deuteronomy we read, "Do not say to yourself, 'My power and the might of my own hand have gotten me this wealth.' But remember the LORD your God, for it is he who gives you power to get wealth, so that he may confirm his covenant that he swore to your ancestors, as he is doing today" (Deut. 8:17, 18).

Charles R. Lane, director of the Center for Stewardship Leaders in St. Paul, Minnesota, cautions that preachers need to be careful how we use the word *gift* to describe all that people receive from God, because God does not give gifts in the way we understand and use this word.[3] God does not give things to us in the sense that we then own them and are free to do whatever we please with them. Instead, God entrusts everything we are and everything we have to us, and God desires, even expects, that we will use everything God entrusts to us according to God's will. Rather than giving us *gifts*, God actually gives us the privilege and responsibility of caring for everything that belongs to God. Instead of asking, "How much should I give to God?" we ask, "How does God want me to use everything?" How does our faith—our relationship with God—influence the way we make use of everything God entrusts to us?

The Bible's answer to the question of how much we are to give to God is really quite simple. We give everything we have and are to God because God already owns everything. Jesus said to someone who asked what he must do to have eternal life, "If you wish to be perfect, go, sell your possessions, and give the money to the poor, and you will have treasure in heaven; then come, follow me" (Matt. 19:21). We have seen that, according to the book of Acts, the first Christians "would sell their possessions and goods and distribute the proceeds to all, as any had need" (Acts 2:45). God has a claim not on one-tenth of our money and possessions but on ten-tenths or 100 percent.

For most people, literally giving 100 percent of what we have to God is impractical and unrealistic. Giving literally everything to God through the church even goes against our responsibility as stewards of the precious things that God has entrusted to us, such as families, friendships, and our capacity to provide for our own lives. Most people cannot give literally everything to the church, and when they do, then often expect the church or someone else to provide for their needs. So how do we give everything to God? Though most of us cannot give 100 percent to God by giving it to the church or giving it away, we all can be certain that our faith influences what we do with everything God entrusts to us. James Hudnut-Beumler reports that Josiah Strong, an early figure of the Social Gospel movement, articulated this universal principle: "Of our entire possessions, every dollar, every cent, is to be employed in the way that will best honor God."[4] Accepting this principle means we can never think that we discharge our responsibility to God by giving a tenth or any other amount short of everything to the Lord. We fulfill our responsibility to God by using everything entrusted to us in a way that honors God. Some stewardship writers go a step further and say, when we accept this principle, the question of how much to give God is turned on its head. Rather than asking, "How much of my money should I give to God?" the question becomes, "How much of God's money do I dare keep for myself?"[5]

Of course, because we are to use everything entrusted to us in ways that honor God, giving to God is larger than and not equal to giving to the church. In fact, we give to God in many ways beyond giving to the church. We obviously give to God when we give to those in need, when we give to organizations that do God's work, and when we use our money responsibly for our families and even for ourselves. Sometimes, giving to the church may not be the best way for us to give to God. For example, according to Mark Allan Powell, the Bible teaches we should not give the church the money we need to care for dependent family members.[6] Jesus said to the scribes and Pharisees: "You have a fine way of rejecting the commandment of God in order to keep your tradition! For Moses said, 'Honor your father and your mother'; and, 'Whoever speaks evil of father or mother must surely die.' But you say that if anyone tells father or mother, 'Whatever support you might have had from me is Corban' (that is, an offering to God)—then you no longer permit doing anything for a father or mother, thus making void the word of God through your tradition that you have handed on. And you do many things like this" (Mark 7:9–13). The author of 1 Timothy writes, "And whoever does not provide for relatives, and especially for family members, has denied the faith and is worse than an unbeliever" (1 Tim. 5:8).

We need to note two important points as we answer the question of how much the Bible says we should give to God. First, giving to the church is only one way we give to God. In fact, giving money to the church is not any holier or more godly than faithfully using our money to pay our bills, send our children to college, provide for aging parents, purchase a needed car or computer, or buy a gift for a loved one. Second, whatever we give to the church, and however we determine what that gift is, it is always only part of what we give to God. On the one hand, we cannot think that, once we give to the church, we fulfill our responsibility to give to God. On the other hand, we must consider all the ways we give to God as we determine how much we will give to the church.

In chapter 5, I said Scripture teaches that giving is to be regular and according to a plan. Paul provided the Corinthian congregation with one plan: "On the first day of every week, each of you is to put aside and save whatever extra you earn, so that collections need not be taken when I come" (1 Cor. 16:2). Scripture provides us with several other plans for giving. These include (1) first fruits giving, (2) proportionate giving, (3) tithing, and (4) growing in giving. As I said in chapter 5, Scripture also teaches that giving is to be voluntary. Paul writes, "Each of you must give as you have made up your mind" (2 Cor. 9:7). The task in the stewardship sermon is to help people make up their minds and give freely. To accomplish this, preachers responsibly provide their congregations all the biblical models, rather than selecting (or neglecting) some of them. We invite our congregations to consider these biblical plans as ways of responding to the gospel and growing in faith. Moreover, preachers present these biblical models responsibly by following the guidelines discussed in chapter 3. In this chapter, I undertake to responsibly provide these biblical models for you.

Give First Fruits

Giving "first fruits" to God means that, whenever we receive income and however we receive income, we give to God first according to our predetermined plan. The opposite of first-fruits giving is first attending to the needs, desires, and obligations of this life and then giving God the leftovers. In Deuteronomy, Moses declares, "When you have come into the land that the LORD your God is giving you as an inheritance to possess, and you possess it, and settle in it, you shall take some of the first of all the fruit of the ground, which you harvest from the land that the LORD your God is giving you, and you shall put it in a basket and go to the place that the LORD your God will choose as a dwelling for his name" (Deut. 26:1–2). While Deuteronomy makes first-fruits giving sound like a command, preachers might share with their congregations the blessings that come from giving to God first. In the same way as we express appreciation for and honor certain people at a dinner by serving them first, first-fruits giving is a way we honor God for all God gives and does for us. Proverbs teaches, "Honor the LORD with your substance and with the first fruits of all your produce" (Prov. 3:9).

Giving first fruits provides a way to cultivate a spirit of contentment with what we have and dependence on God to provide for us. Giving to God first means that we live off the rest. The author of 1 Timothy writes, "Of course, there is great gain in godliness combined with contentment; for we brought nothing into the world, so that we can take nothing out of it; but if we have food and clothing, we will be content with these" (1 Tim. 6:6–8). At first, these words sound naive and even ridiculous. However, over time, as we give to God first, we become more grateful for what we have, and gratitude *for* what we have leads to contentment *with* what we have. Contentment is a way we concretely resist the power of affluence and mammon. Timothy V. Olson observes,

"When we pause to give the first fruits as an act of gratitude, we open a door to live in a very counter-cultural way. We open a door to being satisfied with what we have. We encounter an opportunity to step off the treadmill of having more."[7]

Obviously, giving to God first is key to growing in generosity. We can be more generous when we give out of everything we have rather than giving from what is left. Giving to God first, particularly when we give money away to concretely make a difference in the world, makes us more aware that we participate in God's own work in the world. This awareness is likely to bring us joy and so empower us to give cheerfully. Moses exhorts Israel to "take some of the first of all the fruit" and give it to God for good reason (Deut. 26:2). Still, how much is "some"?

Give Proportionately

The Bible does not mention a specific amount that we are to give. Instead, Scripture tells us to give proportionately according to what we have received. "Then you shall keep the festival of weeks for the LORD your God, contributing a freewill offering in proportion to the blessing that you have received from the LORD your God" (Deut. 16:10). I have already reflected on Paul's testimony that the Macedonian Christians "voluntarily gave according to their means, and even beyond their means" (2 Cor. 8:3). They gave in proportion to what they received, and some gave even more.

Proportionate giving is a sign that Christian communities are committed to egalitarianism. Because giving is to be in proportion to one's assets, everyone gives equally. Those who have much wealth are expected to give proportionally. Those who have little wealth are also expected to give proportionally. In this regard, giving in proportion to our blessings means considering how financially blessed we are compared to others in the community, and not how blessed and generous we feel on any given Sunday. When everyone gives the same proportion, no one gives more or less than anyone else. Because everyone gives eagerly in proportion to their means, those who are able to give much are never to be revered above those who are only able to give a little. Paul calls it "a question of a fair balance" (2 Cor. 8:3, 13).

The good news of giving proportionately is that the size of the gift really does not matter. Paul is not concerned with how much the

Corinthians give. Rather, he is concerned that their "eagerness [to minister to the saints] may be matched by completing it according to [their] means." Paul writes, "For if the eagerness is there, the gift is acceptable according to what one has—not according to what one does not have" (2 Cor. 8:11–12).

Jesus made clear that the proportion, rather than the size, of the gift is what is important when he sat down opposite the treasury, watched the crowd putting money in, and commented to his disciples about a widow and the two small copper coins she put in, compared to the large sums that many rich people contributed. Jesus declared, "Truly I tell you, this poor widow has put in more than all those who are contributing to the treasury. For all of them have contributed out of their abundance; but she out of her poverty has put in everything she had, all she had to live on" (Mark 12:41–44). For those without significant financial resources, proportionate giving is comforting. They know that, from Jesus's perspective, their small gift is incredibly generous. At the same time, those with financial resources cannot take pride in the size of their gifts when their gifts are large in dollar amount but small in terms of percentage. Perhaps the best way to preach proportionate giving is for the preacher to stand with the congregation and let God speak to everyone through these passages. In this way, preacher and congregation hear about the distinctive, even countercultural, nature of the Christian community—and their place in it—together.

Give a Tithe

In Scripture we read, "All tithes from the land, whether the seed from the ground or the fruit from the tree, are the LORD's; they are holy to the LORD" (Lev. 27:30). Elsewhere we find, "Set apart a tithe of all the yield of your seed that is brought in yearly from the field" (Deut. 14:22). Since the nineteenth century, the church has used these verses to advocate a scriptural command, obligation, or opportunity to tithe or give 10 percent of all income to God through the church.[8]

In the nineteenth century, the Protestant church in both the United States and Europe found itself in a situation very much like our own as the church's vision for mission and ministry outstripped its resources. American Protestants looked to the British churches as models of church finance, and so tract societies and denominational agencies reprinted tracts advocating voluntary giving, which became popular resources among clergy and found their way into seminary libraries. These tracts undertook to prove a scriptural rule requiring a tithe of one-tenth of one's income and possessions.

Church leaders knew tithing would be successful only to the degree that preachers convinced themselves and their hearers that tithing was a spiritual law beyond appeal. At various points in time, preachers therefore used different biblical texts to argue in various ways that one-tenth is the amount God has always expected, that the tithe is binding on all people, and that tithing is the only way to finance churches. Some preachers used Leviticus 27:30–33 and Deuteronomy 14:22–29 as proof that the tithe was a law given by God through Moses. Others looked to Genesis 14:17–20 to show the tithe is an eternal command that existed in the time of Abraham.

Abraham made an offering to Melchizedek of a tenth of the spoils he recovered from the kings who had robbed both Lot and the king of Sodom. The name *Melchizedek* literally means "king of the priests," and in the Genesis account, Melchizedek functions principally as a connection to the one true God. Because Melchizedek was a king, probably richer than Abraham, and had done nothing to deserve such tribute, advocates of tithing reasoned that Abraham's payment of a tenth could only be the result of compliance with a preexisting divine ordinance. Thus, these preachers concluded that God ordained tithes as a law for every worshiper before the time of Abraham. Citing Jacob's promise in Genesis 28:22—"all that you give me I will surely give one tenth to you"—advocates of tithing argued Jacob was observing the same divine ordinance that his grandfather Abraham had. Because Jacob was neither Jewish nor Christian, tithing belonged to the religion of the first true followers of the one true God. God therefore commanded tithing as an eternal obligation.

Other preachers presented tithing as a fundamental part of worship rather than an eternal obligation. They asserted that God, as sovereign and redeemer, claims the worship of his people and that the acts of worship appropriate to our relationship with God—prayer, praise, and material offerings—are rooted in that relationship. Prayer is an acknowledgment of dependence on God, and praise is our recognition and adoration of God's perfection. Offerings serve two purposes—to express remorse and offer recompense for sin, and to acknowledge

God's sovereignty. While Christ rendered sin offerings, or sacrifices, unnecessary by his atonement, offerings that acknowledge God's ownership of us and our property are still binding. These offerings are a sign of our dependence on and obligation to God and express our faith, love, and gratitude for material as well as spiritual blessings. According to these advocates of tithing, God not only requires offerings as an act of worship and acknowledgment of God's ownership of all, but God also specifies that a tithe, or 10 percent, is God's everlasting minimum expectation. Moreover, God's wisdom is that, by giving the tithe to the church, the worshiper not only pays honor to God and secures God's blessing but supplies the material means necessary for the work of the church as well.

Still other preachers described the tithe as a debt owed to Jesus Christ, which is to be paid before any other debt. In this regard, the tithe for the church was just the beginning of what church members were to give because, according to 1 Corinthians 16:1–2, Christians were expected to give, in addition to their tithes, freewill offerings according to how they had prospered. Preachers argued on Paul's authority that church members were to support charitable causes beyond the local congregation. Yet, until the obligatory tithe was paid, nothing could be called a gift or freewill offering.

Finally, proponents of the tithe argued that, while advocates of stewardship are correct that all things belong to Christ, God knew giving everything to God would never happen. God therefore commanded the tithe as a means of sensible, conservative, sustainable giving. In fact, the tithe was stewardship's bottom line.

Today, many preachers agree that it is not appropriate to present tithing as a moralistic command, a required act of worship, or a debt owed Christ binding on everyone, as a narrow emphasis on the tithe often does. Some question the theological assumptions and exegetical methods that lie behind these assertions. Others point out that tithing may not be a realistic or even appropriate goal for everyone, including people on fixed incomes during a time of inflation, college and seminary graduates with significant student loans, those receiving unemployment benefits, and people with extraordinary medical bills. Still others highlight the difficulties inherent in translating the tithe from the cultures of the Bible to our own.

Mark Allan Powell notes that the passages in the Bible that deal with tithing envision a cultural and economic situation very different from our own.[9] For example, tithes paid to the temple covered social welfare for the poor, which we pay for through taxes. Powell notes, "the Israelites were never expected to give 10 percent of their income to the temple in addition to giving 33 percent to the government in income tax."[10] In biblical times, tithing was used to support a class of priests forbidden from owning property and engaging in agriculture. This is not the way Protestant congregations compensate their pastors today. Moreover, because people lived freely on the land, they did not have to pay rent or mortgage payments, real estate taxes, and utility bills. Nor did they pay for health insurance. In response to these cultural differences, some advocates of tithing suggest that in American culture, tithing is giving away a tenth of one's disposable income.

Despite these objections, preachers have not abandoned the tithe. Instead, they present tithing as a spiritual discipline we undertake gratefully, an act of resistance, a worthy goal, and a way of participating in God's own work in the world. For example, Timothy V. Olson advocates teaching tithing as a grateful response to God's gracious abundance in our lives and as a spiritual discipline, rather than a requirement. For Pastor Olson, "Tithing, as an acknowledgement of God's abundance and grace, expresses gratitude for what we *have*, not for what we *desire*."[11] Tithing is a way we declare, "I have enough!" Living on nine-tenths teaches us to take better care of all that God entrusts to us. Tithing is also a way we acknowledge that we are blessed to be a blessing and chart a path to living for others, in spite of the cultural call to look out only for ourselves.

Pastor Olson further describes tithing as an act of defiance, because giving away a noticeable portion of what we have before we do anything else sets a pattern of living in opposition to the economic forces that shape us. Episcopal priest and author Robert Farrar Capon provocatively calls preachers to talk about giving in a way far different from conventional fund-raising appeals. Capon invites preachers to say, "Look, you need to give money away in order to sass the system of money back. Let us have some of what you give away, and we'll get rid of it for you in all the crazy ways we can think of."[12] As an act of resistance, tithing defies the cultural impulse to live for one's own desires.

Powell considers tithing "a 'traditional benchmark' or 'worthy goal' for Christians who find it useful to conform their voluntary giving to some external standard."[13] Powell observes that an external standard grounds our giving in habit rather than mood. People who tithe heartily agree. They eagerly recommend tithing to others and have no desire to stop tithing themselves. For these givers, tithing is a natural part of their life of faith—akin to worship, prayer, and personal witness, and freely undertaken rather than commanded and demanded.

Finally, in chapter 4, I said Scripture teaches that the rich share in the kingdom of God—or are banished from it—by virtue of how they treat the poor and needy. Those who teach and practice tithing remind us that, even in a difficult economy, most Americans are rich compared to both the nations of the world and the people of the Bible. Powell observes that most Americans could give away more than 10 percent of their income before taxes and still be rich beyond the wildest dreams of Israelite farmers or Galilean fishermen.[14] Jesus says, "From everyone to whom much has been given, much will be required; and from the one to whom much has been entrusted, even more will be demanded" (Luke 12:48). While some stewardship experts conclude that asking people to give away 10 percent of their income is financially impossible and psychologically extravagant and even incomprehensible, others are equally convinced that, as a standard of giving, the tithe is simply not high enough. All agree that tithing is a way we participate in God's own work of righting the world and claim—not earn—our place in God's kingdom.

While tithing may not be a divine command binding on people of all times and places, the tithe is a long-established practice and tradition in the church. Preachers need to decide how to present tithing, because they do their people a disservice by neglecting it. Emphasizing giving in response to the gospel coupled with questionable exegetical methods and difficulties in transferring the tithe to our context will lead some preachers to dismiss the tithe as a divine command, worship requirement, and debt owed Christ. However, preachers and congregational leaders should not dismiss tithing altogether. Proclaiming the tithe as spiritual discipline, act of resistance, helpful benchmark, and participation in the reign of God provides opportunities for spiritual growth that many congregants will genuinely appreciate. When presenting tithing, it is key that preachers are not manipulative, or people will likely feel they are failing to keep God's timeless command by their chosen level of giving.

Grow in Giving

Scripture teaches that we are to grow in our giving. Were we ever to become satisfied because we attained the helpful benchmark of the tithe and thought we reached the finish line in giving to God, Scripture shows us that we always have room to grow. More than giving a tithe, Zacchaeus sets his own standard for giving at "one half to the poor." Jesus asked the rich man to give everything, and, indeed, the first Christians did.[15] Recognizing that the Bible's answer to the question of how much we should give up is "everything" leads me to hear Paul's words to the Ephesians as an invitation to perpetually grow in giving. Paul writes, "But speaking the truth in love, we must grow up in every way into him who is the head, into Christ" (Eph. 4:15). To "grow up in every way" certainly includes how we use money. As in every other area of the life of faith, Christ Jesus, rather than some biblical standard, is our goal. Standing with you under the word of God, together we hear Paul say, "For you know the generous act of our Lord Jesus Christ, that though he was rich, yet for your sakes he became poor, so that by his poverty you might become rich" (2 Cor. 8:9). Striving to grow "into [Christ] who is the head" through giving is one way we increasingly give in response to the gospel.

Powell proposes that to grow in giving means Christians move from giving proportionately to support their local church community to giving sacrificially—giving beyond what the world considers reasonable. Powell asserts that, in moving from proportionate to sacrificial giving, we no longer experience giving as an obligation but as a joy, an act of worship, participation in God's reign, and a discipline through which the Holy Spirit helps us grow spiritually.[16] Whatever plan we offer our congregations, stewardship sermons should include the invitation to grow in giving in response to the gospel. Stewardship experts report the best way to get people to grow in their giving is to ask. For example, Charles Lane finds that when asked to grow in their giving, many members of a congregation, often 50 percent a year, will increase their financial response.[17] Proclaiming God's invitation to grow sounds so simple, so easy. Yet, many preachers find doing so very hard. In the next chapter, I attempt to uncover why this is so.

AS YOU PREPARE YOUR SERMON . . .

- How did you learn how much to give to God or the church?
- What are the benefits and risks of helping people understand that giving to God is bigger than giving to the church?
- Does your congregation practice first-fruits giving? How might your congregation undertake this as a spiritual practice or Lenten discipline in the way it handles its finances? How might the preacher use the congregation's experience to invite members to undertake first-fruits giving themselves?
- On average, what proportion of their income do members of your congregation give to the church? What do the leaders of your congregation make of this? How might the congregation best receive and discuss this information?
- Do you preach or hear sermons about tithing? Why or why not? What understanding and approach to tithing do you find the most faithful? What understanding and approach do you find most compelling?
- Is an explicit invitation to grow in giving included in the sermons you preach and hear? Why or why not? How would you craft such an invitation?
- What biblical plan(s) for giving ought to be included in this year's stewardship sermon? Why?

CHAPTER 7

Why Is This
Sermon So Hard?

WHEN I AM SITTING in the study, writing—or perhaps reading—a book on preaching about money and giving, the task of preparing and preaching the stewardship sermon feels safe, simple, and straightforward: (1) Define *stewardship*. (2) Preach the gospel. (3) Connect money and giving—or however you define *stewardship*—as a faithful response to the gospel. (4) Invite people to grow in their giving. (5) Give them a plan. (6) Use a tone appropriate to the gospel. Sitting safely in my study writing this book, I find myself eager and excited to preach a stewardship sermon. Then the emotions—both my own and the feelings I anticipate from the congregation—find their way into the mix. Whenever I sit down to prepare a stewardship sermon for a specific congregation, and especially on the Saturday night before I preach it, I feel the knot in my stomach. I find myself asking, "Why is this so hard?"

I learned I am not alone in asking this question. As I indicated in the preface, many preachers and congregants find stewardship sermons difficult and daunting undertakings, whether they are standing in the pulpit or sitting in the pew. Preaching and listening to sermons about money is uncomfortable because they challenge many of our norms and assumptions. Our attitudes about money are such a large part of us that we seldom pause to examine the reasons for and nature of our discomfort. Therefore, as part of preparing the stewardship sermon, preachers and congregational leaders need to sit together and carefully examine the specific norms and assumptions at work in themselves. By

naming these attitudes and bringing them into the open, our norms
and assumptions lose some of their power and may even change.

We learn this truth from Scripture, in both Mark's and Luke's Gospels. While in the region of the Gerasenes, Jesus asks the demons who
possess a man their name (Mark 5:9; Luke 8:30). Naming the demons
gives Jesus power over them. Empowered by Christ and following his
example, in this chapter I name the "demons" that plague me and, I
suspect, many other preachers as we prepare and preach the stewardship sermon—and congregants as they listen. I find that talking about
powers or *demons*, rather than labeling individuals and their beliefs and
attitudes, affords a degree of objectivity that frees people to enter into
conversation less defensively.

Regardless of form, content, and delivery of the stewardship sermon, preaching about money and giving (1) messes with the power of
mammon, (2) fusses with our own fiscal demons, (3) challenges congregational norms, and (4) stirs up possibilities. I therefore organize this
chapter under these four headings. From the perspective of homiletic
theory, these four *demons* or *powers* correspond to the sermon topic,
the preacher, the assembly or congregation, and how the congregation
responds.

Messing with the Power of Mammon

In chapter 4, I discussed the power that money, affluence, or mammon
exerts in our culture, which holds spirits captive and drives everyone to
act on their desire, causing them to acquire more and more. Here, I move
from the culture into the church and describe three ways money opposes the proclamation of the gospel: (1) by framing how we view others
and ourselves, (2) by seeking to silence proclamation and conversation,
and (3) by influencing how sermons are preached and heard. Preaching
about money and giving is truly an act of resistance because, even in the
church, the power that mammon exerts is both real and strong.

Framing Our View

The first way mammon opposes the proclamation of the gospel is by
framing the way we view both others and ourselves. Even in church, when
money frames the way we view others and ourselves, we do not view

others and ourselves through the frame of the gospel. Simply put, everyone uses money to compare themselves to others. Our economic reality determines our place in society; too often money exerts this same power in the congregation's pecking order. When others regard us from a monetary frame of reference, we soon come to view ourselves—and others—the same way.

Money's hold on us is so strong that homiletics professors James R. Nieman and Thomas G. Rogers describe our economic reality "as an internalized experience that is deeply felt."[1] Nieman and Rogers suggest that, regardless of how much money we can claim for ourselves, everyone feels at least five manifestations of this experience—(1) worth, (2) justice, (3) labor, (4) loyalty, and (5) voice.[2] Their examination is much more detailed than the summary I am able to provide here. Still, my point is to identify ways that money, rather than the gospel, frames the way we view others and ourselves.

First, money attempts to frame the way we view others and ourselves by determining our *worth*. Money becomes the criterion that determines whether others accord us dignity and respect or whether we experience shame and failure. Since others use money to determine whether we are worthwhile human beings, we eventually use this same yardstick to measure and define ourselves. Money's definition of worth stands in stark contrast to the gospel's definition of worth. From the perspective of the gospel, we are worthy because Jesus Christ "gave himself for us that he might redeem us from all iniquity and purify for himself a people of his own who are zealous for good deeds" (Titus 2:14).

For many Christians, money's definition of worth and the gospel's definition of worth create a paradox between Jesus's admonition to "strive first for the kingdom of God and his righteousness" (Matt. 6:33) and our own urge to pursue the American Dream. Many hardworking Christians assume they can pursue both but struggle with an inherent tension. On the one hand, they want to prosper and show they are using their God-given talents to maximum effect; on the other hand, they worry that they might be in an idolatrous relationship with their prosperity. Assuming they can serve both God and money, they look to the church not to help them resist or repudiate the power of mammon, but to provide a broad, sweeping, vital vision of how to use affluence in a Christian manner. In the process, they are caught between keeping their money for the sake of mammon and giving it away for the sake of the gospel. In the end, many discover the wisdom of Jesus's words firsthand: "You cannot serve God and wealth" (Matt. 6:24; Luke 16:13).

The second way money frames the way we see others and ourselves is to define *justice* by reinforcing the erroneous notion that everyone gets what they deserve, including their place in the economic pecking order. This notion of justice causes everyone to feel either isolated, because they believe they have only themselves to blame for what they lack, or entitled. People honestly believe they deserve their money because they earned it by their hard work and intelligence. Therefore, no one has the right to tell them what to do with what they have.

The notion that people get what they deserve stands in stark contrast to the gospel proclamation that everything we are and have is entrusted to us by our gracious God. In chapter 6, I recalled words from Deuteronomy as a reminder that even our hard work and intelligence come from God: "But remember the LORD your God, for it is he who gives you power to get wealth" (Deut. 8:18). We do not have the right to do with our money whatever we choose. On the contrary, we find throughout the entire Bible that those who are wealthy have the duty to give generously of their wealth to alleviate the suffering and improve the conditions of those who are in physical need. Perhaps we should not talk about "giving back to God" since to do so implies what we put in the offering plate is God's and everything else is ours and we can do whatever we want with it.[3] Mammon might understand giving this way. The gospel does not.

The third way money attempts to frame how we view others and ourselves is by defining us according to our *labor*. "What do you for a living?" we ask upon meeting someone. Our identities are summed up in our labor, occupation, or profession, rather than in our personalities, passions, values, and commitments. Once we learn what people do, we quickly and unconsciously determine their worth. We also judge people's character and lifestyle by what they do with their money. Ultimately, the value we assign people based on their labor is determined monetarily. The more money people earn, the more they are worth. Yet, James exhorts, "Listen, my beloved brothers and sisters. Has not God chosen the poor in the world to be rich in faith and to be heirs of the kingdom that he has promised to those who love him?" (James 2:5). God does not define us according to the worth of our labor, but because Christ chose us.

The fourth way money frames the way we view others and ourselves is by the influence our financial resources exert over our *loyalty* to social organizations, including the church. Those with economic privilege treat social organizations as trustworthy and beneficial; they often feel that people who belong to and support social organizations are better than people who do not. Those who are economically vulnerable experience themselves as marginalized from these organizations and even treated by them with suspicion and disdain. Those on the margins end up with a marginal interest in belonging. For those on the margins, what some consider erratic and uncommitted participation is what Nieman and Rogers call "the select loyalty . . . reserved for those already proven to be trustworthy, like family and friends."[4]

The final way money frames how we view others and ourselves is by influencing how we claim our *voice*. We know that people with more economic resources are usually given greater voice than those without. But money also shapes our voice. For example, because people with money have garnered success and accomplishment through their thoughts and ideas, they therefore tend to view faith in God as something to be understood. By contrast, people who are economically vulnerable tend to approach faith in God as the focus of hope and trust rather than understanding. Those who approach God intellectually sometimes regard people emotionally connected to God as naive and uninformed. Those who claim an emotional connection with God may regard those who approach God intellectually as removed and even uncommitted. By framing the way we view others and ourselves, money challenges the gospel frame of reference that frees and empowers us to give.

A Private Matter

A second reason money exerts power in the church is we *consider money a private matter*. Even in families, people do not discuss what they earn and how they spend their money. Privacy or secrecy is a mighty weapon. Charles Campbell argues the powers of death at work in the world, including mammon, aggressively use tactics such as negative sanctions, rewards and promises, and surveillance and secrecy, rebel against God by making idols of themselves and placing their own desires above God's purpose for humanity and creation.[5] In many congregations, the secrecy that surrounds money and giving leads many

Christians to afford money power by regarding giving as a strictly private matter between an individual and God. As we will see, congregants and pastors use Christian values to preserve the secrecy that surrounds money and legitimize their reluctance to talk about what they give. For example, they maintain their secrecy because they do not want to be perceived as either boasting or shaming others. The secrecy that surrounds money then becomes normative.

When preachers address money and giving in sermons and leaders openly discuss money and giving in the congregation, people empowered by money's claim of secrecy get uncomfortable. They may experience preaching about money and giving as invasive, especially if the preacher moves from annually fund-raising from the pulpit to regularly preaching about using money as a faithful response to the gospel and an expression of Christian faith and discipleship. Rather than resolving their discomfort by allowing Scripture to inform their assumptions, they may attempt to enlist Scripture to justify those assumptions.

In one congregation, for example, when I suggested visits with every member of the congregation to discuss stewardship, people quickly quoted Jesus's teaching about giving alms in the Sermon on the Mount as a way of justifying why we should not. Jesus said, "But when you give alms, do not let your left hand know what your right hand is doing, so that your alms may be done in secret; and your Father who sees in secret will reward you" (Matt. 6:3–4). People argued that money should not be discussed in church, because the way people use their wealth is a private matter between them and God, and giving should be secret. Some even argued that giving records must be kept from the pastor to prevent the pastor from ministering to people according to what they give.

As I have said repeatedly, Jesus had much to say about how we are to use money. Here I add that most of what Jesus said about money contradicts our assumptions. For starters, I cannot find anywhere in the Gospels where Jesus asks people to give a portion of their money to fund his ministry and support his church and tells them to keep the rest. Rather than asking us to give some money for the work of the gospel, Jesus is concerned with what we do with all the money we have.

Second, when Jesus says that we should give alms in secret, Jesus is talking about our motivation for giving rather than the practice of giving, a distinction many Christians gloss over. Jesus teaches against drawing attention to our giving so that others might praise us. Jesus is not saying money and giving are private matters, not to be discussed in the Christian community. Jesus's own example makes this clear. Mark tells us that Jesus sat down opposite the treasury and watched the crowd putting money into the treasury (Mark 12:41). Jesus—and everyone else—saw who put money into the treasury and how much. Rather than viewing the offering as a private matter, Jesus seems to consider it a public event, which everyone can witness.

Jesus surely challenges and calls into question our norms and assumptions about money and giving. Preaching is an effective way to help people to realize this. Sometimes, the best way for a congregation to realize Jesus's view of money differs from theirs is for the preacher to let Jesus do the talking by situating the congregation within the biblical narrative. In his sermon "The Widow's Offering" (Mark 12:38–44), Donald P. Kreiss, pastor of Antioch Lutheran Church in Farmington Hills, Michigan, helps "listeners to reflect on what it would be like if the modern practice of 'giving in secret' were to become a more public act, and Jesus were physically present to comment during that process."[6] Dr. Kreiss uses humor to contrast the elaborate rituals and complex decisions involved in "giving secretly" as we put an offering envelope into the plate. Do you write your name and the amount on the envelope? Put it in the plate face-up or face-down? And if you give electronically, or by stock transfer, or once a month, "do you smile bravely and pass, or go ahead and slip a couple of dollars into an envelope, so that your neighbors in the pew will not think you're a deadbeat?"[7] Pastor Kreiss observes that, in Mark's story, there is no expectation of privacy; the amount of money given was a matter of public interest and comment:

And according to Mark, Jesus takes a seat "opposite the treasury" (think: large, metal box designed to receive donations from the faithful). And that part is fine. It is certainly appropriate for Jesus and his disciples to be in the Temple, and Jesus is certainly entitled to sit down wherever and whenever he needs to. But what Mark wants us to know is that Jesus did not simply grab the first open seat, rather, he chose the spot in order to "watch the crowd putting money into the treasury." Yes. That's what Mark says, and he mentions it as though there were seats deliberately placed so that—if one chose, if anyone chose—it was possible to

keep an eye on the proceedings, so as to be able to observe both the do-
nor and the size of the donation going into the box. Can you imagine? . .
. [Jesus] went to the Temple, watched while folks came forward to make
their offerings, and made public comment to his disciples.[8]

Pastor Kreiss then discusses Jesus's commentary on both the rich people and the widow's giving. He suggests that Jesus invites us to consider what it would mean for us to give like the widow, sacrificially rather
than out of our abundance, and candidly observes that, although times
in the congregation's community were far from good, some members
of the congregation still had the luxury of choosing what to do with
their money. Pastor Kreiss then invites the congregation into a vision
of what a small increase in giving—five dollars per week per household—could mean for the life and ministry of the congregation. In this
way, the preacher invites the congregation into the biblical narrative
to experience the difference between Jesus's regard for money and
their own.

How We Preach and Hear Sermons

Finally, money is powerful because *it influences how we preach and hear
sermons*. According to Nieman and Rogers, people's economic reality
shapes preaching in at least three ways.[9] First, people with more education, higher social standing, and greater economic means tend to give
Scripture different authority because of the way they critically approach
it. They are not afraid to question, argue, or disagree with the Bible,
while people of less socioeconomic standing are more likely to accept
it literally and without question. Second, while people making good
money and with power tend to consider the preacher as just another
person, those in need of hope look to the preacher as the one with the
authority to announce it. Third, those whose economic security is ten-
uous and academic attainment modest prefer sermons that appeal to
concrete situations, personal experience, and effective practices. Those
more affluent and educated value consistent logic, appeals to sources,
and well-thought-out ideas. These differences in listeners provide another reason why preaching about money and giving should not be a
single, annual event. Instead, pastors should preach about money and

giving regularly, intentionally crafting sermons that address the different listeners who make up the congregation.

Fussing with Our Own Fiscal Demons

A second reason the stewardship sermon is difficult to preach and hear is that sermons about money and giving fuss with some of our own financial demons. Preachers and congregants therefore need to intentionally ask themselves, "What makes preaching about money difficult *for me?*" To answer this question, we examine our own values about money and preaching about it. We ask, "How has money shaped—and how does money shape—me?"

To further understand their level of discomfort over preaching and hearing the stewardship sermon, preachers especially compare their values about money and giving to those of their congregations and, of course, to the values of the reign of God. For example, a preacher might be very comfortable preaching about money. However, that same preacher might find the stewardship sermon difficult because money is a taboo subject for the congregation. The preacher does not want to go out of her or his way to anger people and so is reluctant to cross a line. Another preacher might be less comfortable asking the congregation to increase its giving because the church board eliminated all benevolent line items from the budget, and the preacher is concerned that the congregation holding on to every dollar it receives is inconsistent with participating in the in-breaking reign of God. To say so in the sermon places the preacher at odds with the church board.

As they answer the question of how money shapes them, preachers and congregants will consider their socioeconomic status, familial norms, and personal and family financial history. Someone whose family lost their home when he or she was growing up is likely to have norms and assumptions about money different from those of someone whose family always had more than enough money. Whatever their experience, preachers in particular must recognize the pastoral office shapes their economic values for more than theological reasons. Despite the erosion of status that many in society contend the ministry has suffered, pastors' professional identity, education, and, for some pastors, income make preachers socially privileged. Even when pastors' personal background is from a lower class, simply holding the pastoral office relocates them and reinforces new ways of thinking and acting.

Preachers might examine the financial assumptions on which their daily lives rest. Nieman and Rogers suggest several common values, basic goals for human striving, that symbolize blessing and even privilege when attained and failure and even worthlessness when not achieved.[10] These values are order, health, security, and hope. First, preachers might explore how much *order* is in their lives. People in comfortable circumstances can assume a level of stability that is constantly under assault in the lives of people lacking financial resources. For example, missing a day of work is less chaotic for a salaried employee than for someone who earns an hourly wage. Preachers might then reflect on their own *health* and the health of members of their congregations. Do people have the financial resources to seek health care and intervention when they are sick? Do they have the financial resources to secure adequate nutrition and shelter so that they do not get sick? Third, how *secure* does the preacher feel? How secure do members of the congregation feel? Do people feel safe, or are they afraid? People whose daily lives are marked by insecurity tend to be conservative rather than risk takers. Because daily life brings its own risks, they need to reduce rather than take on additional risks to get along in the world. Finally, preachers might assess the level of *hope* by considering how they and their hearers view the future. When people's lives are marked by order, health, and security, they are more hopeful.

In addition to these general financial values, preachers need to explore personal demons directly connected to preaching the stewardship sermon. First, what kind of stewardship role model are they? Many preachers feel uncomfortable preaching about money and giving because they know they are not exceptional role models in their own financial stewardship. They feel hypocritical because, although they may know what the Bible teaches about money, they find it easier to preach and teach the Bible than to live according to what the Bible says. In fact, many preachers know themselves to be subject to and complicit with the power of mammon or affluence. Alternatively, preachers can be so committed to giving that they lose touch with the ways growing in giving is a genuine struggle. These preachers may inadvertently become self-righteous like the Pharisee who prayed, "God, I thank you that I am not like other people. . . . I fast twice a week; I give a tenth of all my income" (Luke 18:11–12).

Rather than avoiding preaching about money and giving, preachers help themselves to grow in giving by preaching what the Bible teaches, what they know to be true, to their hearers *and to themselves*, and by trusting that God works through their preaching to empower them to grow as givers. Preachers can also name the challenges of growing in giving. One congregant remarked, "During the first few years of ministry, when they are burdened with student debt, pastors have a unique opportunity to speak authentically to the struggle to be a faithful steward." Most important, preachers remember that God and not the preacher is the focus of the sermon.

Many pastors are uncomfortable preaching the stewardship sermon because they are very aware that talking to their congregations about money and asking them to grow in their giving can be perceived as extremely self-serving. This discomfort is not without cause. The pastor's salary and benefits make up the largest single category in most congregations' budgets. Congregants can further increase the preacher's anxiety with not-so-subtle remarks, such as, "You didn't go into the ministry to make money—did you, pastor?" Even pastoral colleagues can make a preacher feel anxious and ashamed for taking an "extravagant" vacation, wearing an "overly expensive" suit of clothes, or enrolling her children in a private school.

The New Testament expects the people will support their ministers. In 1 Corinthians, Paul asserts his right as an apostle to food and drink, to a believing wife, and to refraining from doing other work for a living (1 Cor. 9:4–6). Paul writes, "Do you not know that those who are employed in the temple service get their food from the temple, and those who serve at the altar share in what is sacrificed on the altar? In the same way, the Lord commanded that those who proclaim the gospel should get their living by the gospel" (1 Cor. 9:13–14). Preachers need to be unapologetic like Paul. Congregations cost money to operate, and most depend on their members to meet those expenses. A responsibility of belonging to a congregation is supporting it financially. The question, of course, is whether the pulpit is the appropriate place to have this conversation.

Another way preachers lessen their discomfort is by coming to terms with the financial implications of the nature of the pastoral call and the realities facing the church. Understanding the history of clergy compensation in the United States over the last two hundred years is helpful for this purpose.[11] First, the evangelical conception of a minister as one who pours out his life for the gospel, which began with Methodist circuit riders making less than one hundred dollars a year in the early nineteenth century, has continued as a romantic ideal down to this day. Throughout the past two hundred years, Protestant clergy were more comfortable with the idea of having a calling than of belonging to a profession. As a consequence, pastors willingly accepted compensation that a more professionally minded group in society would not. Even when offered the chance to receive more money, some clergy rejected this opportunity as unchristian. More recently, preachers embraced the mantle of servant leaders, with the result that in the year 2000, we found ourselves paid in many places as servants. If a pastor is not willing to serve in those circumstances, usually some other pastor or, increasingly, a lay leader is. The ideal of the pastor pursuing a calling rather than an income together with a ready supply of replacements for clergy who ask for too much money are enduring features of American Protestant church life.

Second, increased lay leadership of congregations has had a dampening effect on setting pastors' salaries, particularly when lay leaders come from a wider range of economic backgrounds than has been previously true and when they use the same market calculus for setting pastors' salaries that they are subjected to in their places of work or retirement. During periods of price or wage instability, clergy historically receive reduced incomes for the same work they previously performed. As is true in their own lives, congregational leaders have come to count on their pastors belonging to a two-earner household and having fewer children to buffer the drop in ministers' real wages.

Third, preachers' salaries are also affected by the church's response to the loss of its members. Mainline churches have given up significant numbers of members but have not closed many congregations. The result has been congregations of fewer people still trying to support a ministry and a minister. Today, ministry is one of the few fields whose members can expect negative income returns to advanced education. That is, pastors earn less after attending seminary than had they never gone and chosen some other work. While other industries and professions can boost wages by increasing productivity, most congregations of a few hundred people on average cannot use this approach by significantly increasing worship attendance, though many congregations embrace evangelism for precisely this purpose. Ministers who do get ahead economically for a sustained period after their midforties generally do so by moving to more remunerative posts and not by receiving larger salaries from the congregations they serve.

A preacher's own values about money, personal practice of giving, and willingness to preach about a subject that affects them personally all contribute to the level of anxiety he or she experiences when preparing and preaching the stewardship sermon. These demons also complicate how the congregation hears and receives the stewardship sermon. Preachers and congregations will therefore intentionally attend to these matters. Yet, managing the discomfort that may surround the stewardship sermon involves more than inner work. Preachers must learn congregational norms about money so as not to be caught by surprise when the stewardship sermon challenges those norms.

Challenging Congregational Norms

I know people who expect that a wedding sermon will reveal something embarrassing about the couple, that a funeral sermon will include a eulogy, and that God will take a back seat in the Mother's Day sermon. In this regard, the stewardship sermon is like a wedding, funeral, or other special-occasion sermon. Congregants bring all sorts of expectations with them when they come to hear it. Remaining oblivious to those expectations can be like wandering through a minefield, because the preacher never knows when he or she will misstep and set off an explosion in the congregation. To release this anxiety, preachers discover what norms and values surround conversation about money in the congregation. Preachers are then aware of when the stewardship sermon challenges those norms and can determine how to deliver that challenge and deal with any fallout.

One way pastors might uncover congregational norms about money is by analyzing the ages of its members. Homiletics professors Joseph R. Jeter Jr. and Ronald J. Allen, writing in 2002, assert that most congregations today are made up of people from four generations, which they call builders, silents, boomers, and generation 13.[12] I add a brief discussion of Generation Y to Jeter and Allen's analysis.

As their name suggests, *builders* (born 1901–1924) build social institutions that stave off deprivation and violence, construct community, and provide for progress. They work very hard in the church and other institutions to which they belong. Builders are interested in the church's financial solvency. They are loyal to God, feel a strong sense of obligation, and respond well to a challenge. This generation is receptive to giving out of their obligation to God.

Silents or the silent generation (born 1925–1942) yearn to believe that their lives and their works have mattered to the human community and to God. They have a deep, strong, and tender commitment to justice. Silents respond well to sermons that articulate a vision and describe how Christians can put that vision into practice in specific situations. In this way, the preacher helps silents recognize points where their lives cohere to the gospel and points where the gospel calls them to be more just. Giving as participation in the reign of God and as resistance to the powers are ways to approach this generation.

Boomers (born 1943–1960) experience the church as not making a significant enough difference for them to support it with their time, energy, and money. They can support their values and causes of choice without the burdens of institutional religion. They yearn for a vision that will help them understand life as a whole. They seek a distinctly Christian way of interpreting the world. Boomers desire sermons that deal with real life issues without bullying or obligation. Preachers can help boomers recognize the connection between Christian vision and its call to witness through specific actions, including giving. Preachers can also help boomers understand the particular ways God works through the congregation and church. Since boomers value experiential sermons, preachers will point to concrete experiences of the congregation and church participating in God's own work in the world.

Generation 13 (born 1961–1981) is the first generation in the history of the United States to expect a lower standard of living than that of its parents. They turn to personal experience for authoritative guidance on spiritual matters. Preachers can help this generation understand the gospel's eschatological vision in terms of money and giving. Preachers need to be honest and authentic, and do well to share the struggles of giving. Preachers can also appeal to corporate identity and the need to nurture community.

Generation Y (born 1982–2001), also called the millennial generation, is characterized by an increased use and familiarity with communications, media, and digital technologies. Members of generation Y filter, sort, prioritize, eliminate, and process more marketing messages than just about any other population group in existence. This generation exhibits a deep trust in authority and institutions, is somewhat conventional in its approach, and depends on teamwork. Yet, it is nonetheless powerful in its energetic, decisive, and strong leadership. This generation is willing to trade the fast track for a better balance between work and life. Since their economic prospects are uncertain, they tend to be frugal. On the one hand, members of this generation believe in God, pray, and attend worship. On the other, they regard the church as sexist, homophobic, and xenophobic. This generation contributes to causes to which they have a personal connection and that make an obvious difference in the world.

A second way preachers might uncover congregational norms about money is to explore the piety that surrounds giving. For example, as I have said, many Christians believe how much someone gives is between that person and God. Church leaders therefore have no right to tell people how much to give or to request pledges. Alternatively, Lutheran theologian T. A. Kantonen asserts that, from the perspective of the gospel, to ask "What should I give?" or "How much should I give?" indicates spiritual immaturity coupled with legalistic calculation, rather than the overwhelming spontaneity of faith that works through love. Kantonen writes, "It is the same type of question as Peter's question, 'How often should I forgive my brother?' (See Matthew 18:21–22). On that level, 'one-tenth' is as reasonable an answer to the question of giving as Peter's suggestion of 'seven' is to the question of forgiving. The Lord's answer to Peter's question, 'Not seven, but seventy times seven,' indicates that his answer as to how much to give would be, 'Not one-tenth but ten times one-tenth.'"[13] Still others consider both preaching about money and asking congregants to pledge to be indications that the pastor and congregational leaders lack faith. More than once a parishioner reminded me that Scripture presents Abraham as a model of faith. These parishioners then reminded me that

Abraham declared, "The LORD will provide" (Gen. 22:14). The church member then says, "Pastor, you just need to have a little faith." This piety presumes the purpose of stewardship is to raise enough money to meet the congregation's budget.

Some Christians believe money is an inappropriate topic for preaching because it is inherently bad, even evil. The New Testament teaches that money and possessions pose a threat to our relationship with Jesus. Money can claim our allegiance and make us forget our responsibility to God and to our neighbor. The more money and possessions a person has, the greater the threat. Yet, while "the love of money is a root of all kinds of evil" (1 Tim. 6:10), Scripture presents money as a good thing. The Gospels recognize possessions are both necessary and good gifts of God. Jesus was not an ascetic, and he did not advocate an ascetic lifestyle for his followers. Walter Pilgrim observes, "Luke's portrayal of Jesus' life depicts a person who rejoices in life and accepts the goodness of God's creation, including some of the things that only money can buy."[14] Jesus knew people of wealth and spent time with them. He enjoyed banquets with good food and drink. In fact, Jesus's favorite image of the coming age was the Messiah and all the redeemed sharing the heavenly feast, where supreme joy reigns.[15]

In Matthew's Gospel, Jesus says, "If you then, who are evil, know how to give good gifts to your children, how much more will your Father in heaven give good things to those who ask him!" (Matt. 7:11). Mark Allan Powell observes that, in the Gospels, these "good things" include "nice clothes and jewelry (Luke 15:22), fatted calves (Luke 15:23), casks of wine (John 2:6–10), perfume (Mark 14:3–6), houses and fields (Mark 10:30) and other things associated with pleasant living in a very material world."[16] Money is not an end in itself. The acquisition of money is not to dominate our lives. Jesus asks, "What does it profit them if they gain the whole world, but lose or forfeit themselves?" (Luke 9:25). Jesus declares, "Take care! Be on your guard against all kinds of greed; for one's life does not consist in the abundance of possessions" (Luke 12:15). This is certainly an appropriate subject for a sermon!

Some Christians believe preaching about money and giving is inappropriate because the financial life of the congregation is separate from the spiritual life of the congregation. For some, the implicit message is that the congregation's financial life is inferior to the congregation's spiritual life. It should be handled quietly by a small group of people with financial and business expertise and discussed publicly only when necessary. Others feel that sound financial and business principles— rather than Scripture, which governs the congregation's spiritual life— govern the congregation's financial life. For both these reasons many pastors and congregations hold that pastors should confine themselves to spiritual matters and not be involved in the financial life of the congregation. Some people feel this is especially true because, while pastors possess the wisdom and expertise to guide the spiritual life, they are not trained in business and therefore are not qualified to participate in the "business side" of the church. In many congregations, this view persists even when the pastor had a pervious career in business.

Accepting a distinction between a congregation's spiritual and financial ministries means that people do not have to examine either their personal financial lives or congregational financial lives from the perspective of the gospel or in light of Scripture. Keeping the pastor out of the congregation's financial life is also a way some members exercise power and hang on to control. They do not want their pastor involved in congregational stewardship and finances because they do not want the pastor to know what people give, to discover that congregational giving is not what it should be, or to change how the congregation handles stewardship and finances. In response, Powell correctly observes, "Church leaders need to know the giving levels of their parishioners for the same reason that physicians need to know certain 'vital signs' for their patients—financial giving is one key indicator of spiritual health."[17]

Finally, preachers might explore how members of the congregation understand the relationship between giving and the congregation's mission. People hold different assumptions about what the church ought to be doing and what they ought to be expected to pay for. For example, some church members are convinced that preaching about stewardship undercuts evangelism. They can vividly recall other congregations in which sermons and direct appeals left the impression that "all the church is interested in is money." They therefore insist that Jesus, rather than money, be the subject of the sermon, and that the congregation make it clear that visitors are not expected to contribute. We have seen that the New Testament is concerned that congregations support their ministers, provide for members of the congregation who are in need, give money to other congregations in distress, and finance sharing the good news of Jesus with the world. Pastors and congregational leaders need to make clear how money entrusted to the church relates to these New Testament priorities and the gospel.

Pastors and congregational leaders also need to clearly distinguish between stewardship and paying the church's bills. Powell asserts the greatest misconception regarding financial stewardship in Christian congregations today is that people believe they are answering God's call to sacrificial renunciation by simply fulfilling a basic expectation of responsible church membership.[18] Powell argues that people choose to worship with a particular congregation and participate in its programs because they want a pastor and the benefits from the ministry that pastor provides. They want the congregation to grow in the community and the values it represents to grow in the world. They therefore give money to the church to pay the mortgage and the pastor's salary and provide for program expenses. Powell says, "It is good and responsible that people make donations to cover these expenses—they would be wrong *not* to do so—but they are not really *giving away* their money in a sense that matches the biblical call to radical renunciation. What they are doing is fulfilling what should be a reasonable and obvious expectation of church membership—they are doing their part to sustain the life and mission of a community to which they belong."[19] Powell rightly nuances his statement by noting that congregations spend a significant portion of their money on benevolence—programs and activities from which a congregation's own members might not directly benefit—and that any given member will find her or his contribution pays expenses for things from which she or he does not directly benefit. Yet, Powell nevertheless insists that we not confuse "fulfilling an expected, reasonable commitment to our local congregation and *giving away our money* in a spirit of sacrificial renunciation."[20] He believes the richest spiritual blessing comes in the move from giving what is reasonable to giving what this world considers radical. As we make this move, God's goodness takes hold of our lives and transforms us according to the gospel.

Stirring Up Possibilities

Thinking about God's goodness taking a hold of our lives and transforming us according to the gospel certainly stirs up possibilities for both preachers and congregational leaders. Because preachers and congregational leaders give to the church in large part because they believe in the work the church is doing—participating in God's own work in the world and resisting the powers of death that are opposed to God— they cannot help but imagine how much more the church could do to further the gospel if more members were inspired to give more generously. Alternatively, preachers and congregational leaders may fear that, if the stewardship sermon is unsuccessful, people will give even less than they have been giving, and the congregation's ministry will be diminished, if not put in jeopardy. Whether the cause is fear or hope, the stewardship sermon at some level stirs up expectations that can heighten anxiety for both those who preach and those who hear.

What can we realistically expect the stewardship sermon to achieve? As part of his economic history of the Protestant church in North America, James Hudnut-Beumler asked whether efforts to preach the righteousness of tithing in its various forms worked. He explored the extent to which preaching stewardship was successful as measured by congregants' behavior. Hudnut-Beumler found, for example, that at the turn of the twentieth century, contemporary reports revealed congregations only partially accomplished their intended results, even those that had been offered as examples of great success. Three congregations hailed as models of success boasted that 9.9, 12.5, and 17 percent of their members practiced tithing.[21] Nevertheless, the increase in giving accomplished by this partial success was dramatic enough to give pastors and congregational leaders hope for all that their congregations might do to further the work of the gospel. "If every member of this church would tithe, we could . . ."

Historically, preachers and church leaders compared the number of members who tithed with those who did not, and they assumed, were it not for preaching on tithing, everyone would give at the same low level as those who did not tithe. This is not true. Generous people are generous. In fact, rather than creating new tithers, preaching about tithing has, in most cases, simply moved highly committed and generous church members to become marginally more generous. In the places where it was perceived to work, tithing was more important for boosting the mood of the congregation than it was for improving the bottom line in the short term. Hudnut-Beumler observes, "A congregation in which some were willing to sign a tithing covenant and actually give a tenth of their incomes to the church was bound to be a congregation in which a critical mass of parishioners had a stake in the success of the mission."[22] Statistics suggest that in 1920 American Protestants as a group, rather than giving a tithe, were allocating 3 percent of their pretax gross incomes to their churches. Hudnut-Beumler concludes, "A half century of preaching and teaching the tithe, and of framing Christian attitudes toward possessions under the rubric of stewardship, had not produced a nation of Protestant tithers. Nor had that half century of effort dimmed the clergy's hopes that their people might yet be more generous."[23]

This trend continues today. Hudnut-Beumler reports statistics from the George Barna organization and the Southern Baptism Convention that indicate that, in the early years of the twenty-first century, even in evangelical churches, 80 percent of giving to the church comes from 20 percent of the people, just as in mainline congregations, while up to 50 percent of the members of evangelical churches give very little or not at all. In mainline churches, the average church member gives 2 to 3 percent of his or her income to the church, and roughly 25 percent of church members give financially little or nothing.[24]

Research also indicates that, after years of hearing stewardship theology from the pulpits, most members of the business class continue to operate from the perspective of finance rather than the gospel. In fact, while pastors and some congregational members use biblical and theological arguments for giving, others, including congregational leaders, are in favor of using sound business principles and proven fund-raising techniques to govern how the church raises and spends its money. In other words, each group advocated the approach it finds most compelling.

This research indicates that a congregation's deficit woes, if not the deficit itself, will not disappear because of a single stewardship sermon. Nor will a congregation's ministry be destroyed if that sermon misses the mark. Preachers and church leaders should therefore be clear about what the sermon will and will not accomplish.[25] Preaching works well for what Ronald A. Heifetz, director of the Leadership Education Project at the John F. Kennedy School of Government, Harvard University, calls adaptive work. According to Heifetz, *adaptive work* consists of "the learning required to address conflicts in the values people hold, or to diminish the gap between the values people stand for and the reality they face."[26] Adaptive work is distinct from *technical work*, the work organizations and their leaders undertake when a problem is clear and both the solution and the means of implementing it are obvious. Preaching is a less effective means of leadership in these situations. However, when defining the problem and identifying and implementing a solution depend upon people learning new values, attitudes, and habits of behavior, preaching is an effective way to lead congregations in this adaptive work. Preaching articulates how the gospel informs and shapes our attitudes and actions, including those involving money and giving. Preaching seeks to help people frame money and giving using the gospel and identify all possible faithful responses, so that individual members and the congregation as a whole can discern together which is best. Rather than causing an instantaneous change, preaching works slowly but effectively to change people's values, attitudes, habits, or behavior.

Preaching about money and giving should therefore have a long-term perspective and not be confined to meeting the requirements of the annual budget. Nora Tubbs Tisdale encourages preachers to take the long view and not think that change in people and in the congregation happens either instantaneously or not at all.[27] The absence of a dramatic increase in giving indicates neither that the congregation is obstinate nor the preacher ineffective. Rather, change in people happens slowly and imperceptibly over time. When it comes to money and giving, and many other concerns for that matter, preachers and church leaders do better to think of the cumulative effect of preaching, the small but significant ways sermons change people and faith communities over weeks, years, and lifetimes. Just as one snapshot has a minimal influence on the observer's view of the subject but a collection of artistic photographs can change one's perspective, so the single sermon rarely transforms the lives of those who hear it, but consistent gospel preaching over seasons of individual and congregational lives has the power to deepen faith and change behavior. As is true for helping Christians to grow in prayer, Bible study, and service to the neighbor, the cumulative effect of small, transforming conversions makes preaching about money and giving an immensely important part of the ministry of the church.[28]

Finally, as is true for so many practices of Christian faith, preaching about money and giving needs to be partnered with other opportunities and activities. By the end of World War II, fund-raising techniques in Protestant church circles had been honed to businesslike precision. The majority of books about church finances concerned technique rather than theology. This trend continues today, as the stewardship sermon is partnered with mailings, meals, meetings, and an array of other activities in an annual stewardship emphasis or campaign. The partnership of preaching and aspects of the stewardship campaign is the subject of our final chapter.

AS YOU PREPARE YOUR SERMON . . .

- How are you feeling as you prepare to preach or hear the stewardship sermon? What is the mood of the congregation?
- Name one way that money frames the way you view yourself and someone else. Name one way that money does not. Name one way your congregation uses money to frame itself and others. How does the gospel challenge or refocus this frame?
- How openly is money discussed in your congregation? How might this attitude affect giving?
- How has money shaped—and does money shape—you? How might this make preaching about money difficult for you?
- What expectations do you and the members of your congregation have of the stewardship sermon? Are they realistic? Are they based on the gospel or something else?
- What piety surrounds your giving and giving in your congregation?
- How would you describe the relationships among money, giving, and mission in your congregation?

CHAPTER 8

What Else
Can We Do?

IN CHAPTER 1, I OBSERVED that, for good and for ill, the steward-ship sermon is never a solo act, because it is always tethered with some sort of fund-raising technique—in church talk, the stewardship campaign or annual response program. In many congregations, the annual stewardship program, "that time each year when members of the congregation are asked to consider the blessings God has entrusted to them and how they will respond to those blessings through financial support of the church,"[1] is the cornerstone of stewardship ministry. For preachers, this is good news, because other activities aimed at relating faith and money and getting people to give prevent the preacher from either assuming all responsibility or being held solely responsible for raising the congregation's finances. Everything does not rest on the annual stewardship sermon.

Preachers do need to assume two responsibilities for the stewardship campaign in addition to preaching gospel-centered stewardship sermons. First, in the planning process, the preacher is responsible for guaranteeing that the gospel guides whatever fund-raising techniques the congregation uses. Second, during the campaign, the preacher is responsible for working with congregational leaders to hold the stewardship program accountable to the gospel that is preached. Together, preachers and congregational leaders ensure that preaching and the congregation's stewardship campaign complement rather than contradict each other. When preaching the gospel and the stewardship campaign work together, the proclamation of the gospel is amplified. When the sermon becomes the means or occasion to sell the stewardship program or to appeal to people to give using fund-raising techniques, preaching—and even the gospel—is undermined or diminished.

In this chapter, I briefly review some of the projects and activities many congregations include as part of the annual stewardship campaign and how they might be faithfully and successfully partnered with preaching about money and giving in response to the gospel. In some congregations, the stewardship campaign has remained unchanged for so long that doing something new or different may provide the impetus or leaven for renewal. Congregations ought to consider what programs they have used in the past five years and never use the same program three years in a row. After reviewing components of a stewardship program or campaign, I then turn to three facets of stewardship campaigns that are often incorporated into the worship service: testimony, Loyalty or Consecration Sunday, and the offering or collection. Because the weekly offering or Sunday collection is the church's most regular and tangible way of connecting money and giving and the Christian faith, I consider this aspect of worship in the greatest detail.

The Stewardship Campaign

In the course of their history in North America, Protestant churches have collected a cornucopia of components from which congregations can choose as they annually assemble their stewardship campaign. Since World War II, common features of annual stewardship campaigns include pledging, providing members of the congregation literature in advance of asking them to pledge, encouraging members to "step up" or increase their giving, a campaign mentality, congregational leaders making appeals or offering testimonials from the pulpit, the Sunday for pledging, and rituals designed to increase participation. Here I briefly comment on (1) offering envelopes, (2) Sunday school lessons, (3) every-member visits, (4) pledge cards, (5) bulletin inserts, and (6) the fellowship meal. Though the church has retained these techniques, at least in vestigial form, one of the reasons giving to the church has declined since World War II is that few church leaders in mainline Protestantism since World War II have possessed "the confidence (or perhaps audacity) necessary to 'work them' as ably or as shamelessly as religious leaders did in the 1940s and 1950s."[2] Attitude and commitment are key ingredients in any successful stewardship program.

As congregations decide what elements to include in their steward-ship program, leaders should carefully weigh whether the congregation possesses the resources, human and otherwise, to carry those elements out successfully. Testimony, for example, requires people willing and able to effectively testify. Undertaking anything more than providing bulletin inserts or other literature and passing out offering envelopes requires careful planning, committed leadership and volunteers, and a program for follow-up with members of the congregation who do not participate in the program.

Offering Envelopes

I distinctly remember that when I was confirmed, before hands were laid on my head and prayers were said over me, my classmates and I received boxes of envelopes and were told about our responsibility as church members to give to the church. While it was a surprise in the moment, upon reflection this was nothing new. We had been given smaller envelopes all the way through Sunday school. Yet, a new level of seriousness about giving accompanied the adult offering envelopes we received as we prepared to be confirmed.

Offering envelopes serve at least three purposes. First, they encour-age personal rather than family or household giving, because every member of the congregation has his or her own envelopes. Second, en-velopes remind members to contribute regularly, if not weekly. When I was a full-time parish pastor and took the Lord's Supper to homebound members each month, several of the people I visited gave me four enve-lopes with their offerings in them. The congregational treasurer asked me to tell these people that one check in one envelope was more ef-ficient. My wise homebound members were clear that efficiency is not the point. They reported that filling out their offering envelope and putting money in it each week was an act of worship and devotion they could continue as they always had, even though they could no longer come to church. I wonder if something is lost with the efficiency of direct deposit to the church's checking account. Third, offering enve-lopes encourage generosity. The average church member gives a great deal more by giving just a bit at a time and by putting something in the envelope every week, rather than trying to save up a significant sum each year or predetermining the amount that will be deducted from a checking account each month.

Congregational leaders might consider how offering envelopes are distributed to congregational members each year and what implicit or explicit messages are associated with their distribution. In their sermons, imaginative preachers might include reflection on writing one's name on and filling the envelope and placing it in the offering plate each Sunday as a concrete way that we respond to the gospel. Congregation leaders might consider how the stewardship campaign might cultivate an awareness of the ways that placing money in the offering envelope is different from paying another bill.

Sunday School Lessons

John H. Vincent, one of the great figures in the Sunday school movement, believed that the "Sunday school ought to train its members to do" what adult members of the church ought to do.[3] Historically, Sunday school children were taught biblical models of stewardship, the needs of the world, and all the ways they might increase their love of neighbor. Today, we might also say the same about the children's sermon, though research indicates the best use of children's sermons is telling Bible stories in imaginative and engaging ways. For Vincent, teaching children to give necessitated eliminating mixed and questionable motives for giving, which are sometimes at work in Sunday schools. Questionable motives included giving to causes and giving for recognition or reward. As I work with pastors frustrated by a whole host of issues and topics, I find myself repeating the mantra, "They learned well what we taught them." Congregations learn from what the church *does* better than from what the church says or teaches. Congregations lay the foundation for giving by what they do with and teach their children. Leaders must take a long-term perspective and ask what kind of foundation they are laying and what will be the result in ten, twenty, and thirty years. If we teach our children to give to causes, for example, they will give this way as adults.

Every-Member Canvass or Visit

Every adult member of the congregation might receive a visit from congregational elders or leaders who make a personal appeal for support.

For best results, two members of the congregation should visit each individual or family. The visitors deliver a stewardship message or Bible study. They ask those visited to grow in their giving. Finally, the visitors ask all they visit to complete pledge or estimate of giving cards (discussed in the next section), place them in an envelope, and return them to the visitors. Sometimes, the goal of the every-member visit is to ask people to commit to attend meetings or to become members of groups or organizations within the church, trusting that, when people become more involved in the congregation and committed to the work of Christ, their money will follow.

Some congregations assign visitors to people with whom they have a relationship or with whom they share something in common. The relationship or thing in common provides a starting point for the conversation and makes the entire visit easier. Other congregations hold the visits in the church building, where everyone meets on common ground. Visitors might schedule several visits in a single evening. Some congregations do not aim to visit every member every year but have as their goal that every member receives a visit every three years.

The every-member canvass provides God's people with the opportunity to talk about money and giving face to face. The every-member visit not only achieves higher levels of participation when compared to more passive approaches. It also creates a fairly large cadre of leaders who are invested in the program's success and so consider their own giving before visiting others. The large cadre of leaders, of course, is also the program's downside. Visiting every member requires many committed people. If the congregation does not recruit enough visitors, if they are not well trained or lack commitment, the program quickly falls apart.

Congregational leaders and the pastor must do all they can to ensure that the message the visitors bring is gospel centered and biblically based. Well-intentioned visitors sometimes substitute a message they deem more effective, such as giving out of guilt or fear or presenting the congregation as a good investment, which in effect undermines or contradicts the gospel message of the stewardship sermon and program. The goal of these visits is to invite people to grow as disciples of Jesus Christ and not, for example, to scrutinize or defend the congregation's budget.

Pledge or Estimate of Giving Cards

Traditionally, pledge cards are the means by which members of a congregation indicate the amount of money they commit to give to the church in the coming year. Today, pledge cards have become "estimate of giving" cards as a way of subtly making them less obligatory and therefore more inviting. Filling out this card provides an occasion for reflecting on the grace one has received from God and how one wants to respond to that grace. Completing an estimate of giving card involves planning and leads to intentional giving. Completing this card also provides a concrete level of commitment to which one can be accountable. Thus, people who use estimate of giving cards every year tend to increase their giving.

Pledge cards or estimate of giving cards provide congregational leaders with a means for securing a commitment from church members, a gauge for measuring the level of participation in the stewardship campaign, and a concrete reason for the every-member visit—bringing or collecting the pledge card. Pledge cards also help leaders build a realistic congregational budget. Historically, the two-part pledge card and corresponding two-part envelope—one part for congregational expenses and the other for benevolence—put appeals from causes and agencies under congregational control. At the same time, separating congregational expenses from benevolence makes it easier for congregational leaders to forgo giving to benevolence when money is tight and for disgruntled congregational members to give to benevolence and not financially support the congregation—or vice versa.

Despite all their benefits, estimate of giving cards cause some Christians to feel uncomfortable. "I almost feel like they have a negative connotation associated with them," a twentysomething church member commented. "Like, if you give under what you pledge, they hunt you down." Preachers and other church leaders therefore need to be clear that, from a gospel perspective, estimate of giving cards, like offering envelopes, are more than budgetary tools. Pledge cards are primarily a way to help disciples faithfully respond to the gospel. Preachers do better to frame estimate of giving cards as part of a spiritual discipline aimed at helping people to concretely grow in grace. Like committing to reading a chapter from Scripture every day and establishing set times for prayer, completing an estimate of giving card helps us to establish a spiritual habit.

Bulletin Inserts

Congregations include stewardship aphorisms, quotations, and Bible verses in the Sunday bulletin or worship folder, along with the order of worship and announcements of church activities. These stewardship comments, often humorous in nature, are designed to make parishioners think. One example that stuck with me is, "Have you ever seen a hearse pulling a U-Haul?" Another example is more thought provoking than funny: "There is enough of the Lord's money in the wallets and purses of Christians on Sunday morning to do all the work God expects them to do—if God could only get his hands on it!" A third example has a hint of fear and warning to it, suggesting that our money will testify concerning us in the final judgment. "Whether our checkbook will be summoned as evidence by the defense or the prosecution depends upon us." Preachers need to see that the stewardship message in the Sunday bulletin is consistent with the gospel preached in the Sunday sermon. For example, the notion that our checkbook will be offered as evidence in the last judgment confuses if not contradicts my preaching that we cannot earn or merit salvation but only receive it as God's gracious gift in Jesus Christ.

Fellowship Meal

A fellowship meal has a proven record for securing a commitment from congregational members. The meal, usually catered, is held either at the church or in a community building. In addition to the meal, congregational members participate in a program on biblical teaching about money and giving and the congregation's ministry, and are given the opportunity to complete their estimate of giving cards. Noting that Jesus fed the five thousand before preaching to them—a claim supported only in John's Gospel, where Jesus gives the discourse on the bread of life after the crowds who ate the loaves and fishes find him (John 6:24–35)—advocates of the fellowship meal are clear that the meal comes first and the pledging afterward, because "good food produces an amiable mood even among the most reserved."[4]

The strength of the fellowship meal is bringing the congregation together for an occasion that is fun, generates goodwill, and fosters community. A meal provides an opportunity to present both biblical teaching on money and giving and an overview of the congregation's ministry in a positive and uplifting atmosphere. The challenge of a fellowship meal is getting people to attend. Because the stewardship campaign comes down to this single, main event, congregational leaders must do all they can to ensure the highest participation possible. Providing good publicity, asking people to make reservations in advance, serving a high quality meal, and implementing strong follow-up with those who do not attend are essential to the success of the fellowship meal.

Some congregations modify the fellowship meal and hold *dessert and prayer* events.[5] Along with eating dessert together, people participate in a program that includes both scriptural teaching on money and giving and reflection on the congregation's mission. The benefits of dessert and prayer include ease of preparation, the possibility that holding multiple events will involve more people, and because each group is a more manageable size, changing the dynamics of the program from presentation to conversation and reflection. As is true of the fellowship meal, the challenge is getting people to attend.

Offering envelopes, Sunday school lessons, every-member visits, pledge cards, bulletin inserts, and fellowship meals are auxiliary to or separate from the worship service. Three additional components of the stewardship campaign—testimonials, Loyalty or Consecration Sunday, and the weekly offering or collection—are part of the worship service and therefore affect and are influenced by preaching more immediately and directly. I turn now to consider these aspects of the stewardship program in somewhat greater detail.

Testimonials

In many congregations, the message of the stewardship campaign is reiterated weekly from the front of the church as congregational leaders give what I know as "Mission Minutes" or "Temple Talks." At their best, these messages from congregational leaders other than the pastor powerfully attest to God's presence, power, and activity in and through the congregation. At their worst, these messages are little more than commercials for the church as a product, delivered by lay spokespeople. In *When God Speaks through You*, I reflect on the sermon as testimony.[6] Anna Carter Florence, who teaches preaching at Columbia Theological Seminary in Decatur, Georgia, from whom I learned this approach to preaching, is clear that, in church history, testimony's greatest asset is that it is a practice of the church open to all believers. All Christians can deepen their own faith and the faith of others by passionately witnessing to Christ through the way they live and express their faith.[7] While the sermon is a unique form of testimony, the testimonials delivered as part of the stewardship campaign are powerful precisely because someone other than the licensed, official preacher gives them.

Florence reminds us that testimony is not "telling your story" or "using personal illustrations." Instead, testimony is a narration of events and a confession of belief; we tell what we have seen and heard, and we confess what we believe about it. In testimonials that are part of the stewardship program, the person bears witness to how she or he sees God working through money, giving, and the congregation's ministry. Because we are talking about God, testimonials given in worship should have Scripture or God's Word at their heart. Some writers suggest selecting a theme verse. All agree that people hearing what God has to say about how we are to use money, possessions, and wealth is essential. Charles Lane strongly warns against putting a congregational budget before people. He argues that budgets cause most people's eyes to glaze over. A budget only motivates a small percentage of the congregation to give and, in fact, limits giving. A 5 percent increase in the congregational budget in effect limits people to a 5 percent increase in giving.[8] Inasmuch as the testimony concerns financial stewardship, the speaker must be comfortable talking about money and giving as an expression of faith.

At its best, testimony communicates the specific, concrete event the speaker witnessed without attempting to coerce or manipulate. The testimony invites the congregation to enter the witness's world and see it as the witness sees it. Testimony rests on faith rather than proof; its aim is to communicate conviction rather than certainty. It is impossible to prove whether a testimony is true or false; one can only believe or reject it. Testimony that is part of a stewardship program includes asking people to grow in their giving. The challenge of testimony, as in preaching, however, is to make this invitation a response to the gospel.

Testimony does not replace the sermon. Many preachers prefer that it precede the Scripture readings and the sermon so that the preacher might refer to (or subtly correct) it during the sermon. In order for the sermon and testimony to complement one another, the preacher might work with the speaker in crafting and reviewing the testimony. In *When God Speaks through You,* I suggest ways parishioners might collaborate with the preacher in creating the sermon.[9]

Loyalty or Consecration Sunday

Loyalty Sunday or Consecration Sunday is "a sacralized occasion for receiving pledges from members and friends of the church."[10] Though other ceremonies may surround it, the highlight of this Sunday is members of the congregation processing forward to place their estimate of giving cards in a basket or on the altar. With good publicity and advanced planning, Loyalty or Consecration Sunday ensures that members of the congregation are present and ready to present their pledges as part of worship. The occasion is planned to emphasize that one is making a commitment in front of God and the church by, for example, using the term *altar* even when the congregation's theological tradition insists there is no *altar* but only a table on which to share the Lord's Supper.

As the name Loyalty Sunday suggests, people commit to give or increase their giving as an expression of their loyalty to the congregation. Loyalty Sunday builds on the fact that, as Lane indicates, for most people, their primary faith or religious relationship is with the congregation rather than with Jesus Christ. Lane asserts that most of us are more likely to talk about the activities of our congregation than the ways Jesus is active in our lives.[11] Historically, the motives for giving out of loyalty, which the preacher or stewardship program promoted, were very personal and included loving your church and wanting to help it, appreciating all that the church does for your children, recognizing that your church stands for the best things in the community, and acknowledging the help and friendship you receive in your church.[12] To make Loyalty Sunday more effective, congregations kept increasingly sophisticated records of past giving in order to motivate givers to demonstrate their loyalty by "moving up" or increasing their giving when possible.

Today, Loyalty Sunday has become Consecration Sunday, as emphasis has shifted from loyalty to the congregation, to responding to and participating in the gospel. Consecration Sunday focuses on the biblical perspective of giving to grow in grace, discussed in chapter 4. As a spiritual discipline, Christians seek to grow spiritually in their relationship with God by supporting the church's mission with a percentage of their income. The need of the disciple to give for his or her own spiritual development is emphasized, rather than the congregation's need to receive. Loyalty to the congregation is replaced by the desire of Christians to unselfishly give as an act of discipleship.

On Consecration Sunday, members of the congregation complete their estimate of giving or pledge card as part of Sunday worship. Usually, a time in the service is designated for worshipers to complete their cards, often following a sermon from an inspiring guest preacher. As on Loyalty Sunday, a processional offering follows, in which members of the congregation bring their estimate of giving cards forward and place them on the altar. A celebratory meal often follows worship, at which the preliminary results of the stewardship campaign are announced.

The chief strength of Consecration Sunday is directly framing completing a pledge or estimate of giving card as an act of worship, discipleship, and spiritual growth. The weekly offering, in effect, extends or continues this act of praise and expression of faith. A second benefit is that more members of the congregation are likely to attend worship than a special stewardship event. Lane observes that this is especially true if advanced publicity is good, the meal is substantial, and people need to make reservations for the meal. The challenge, according to Lane, is that, in most congregations, only about a third of the members are in worship on any given Sunday. With good publicity and a great meal, only 40 to 50 percent are likely to attend. A strong follow-up program is therefore a must.[13]

Loyalty or Consecration Sunday provides the *occasion* or *context* for the sermon. Preachers should help the congregation approach this occasion as a window that provides a fresh perspective on the grace of God, and the grace of God as a window that provides a new vision of and orientation for the occasion.[14] The goal is to help listeners grasp how God's grace is distinctly present in and through the act of placing an estimate of giving card on the altar. The preacher might use biblical images to narrate or describe this worshipful act—Abraham giving Melchizedek a tenth (Gen. 14:20), Israel bringing first fruits into the house of the Lord (Exod. 23:19; 34:22), the people putting their gifts into the temple treasury as Jesus looked on (Mark 12:41; Luke 21:1), the church after Pentecost distributing the proceeds from the sale of their possessions to all according to their needs (Acts 2:44–45), and Paul collecting for the church at Jerusalem (1 Cor. 16:1–3). The sermon can then use these biblical images and narratives to emphasize God's gracious love and everything God is doing for us and for the world, even more than what the members of the congregation are doing. "The sermon, then, will catch, incorporate, and engage listeners with the plot of this out-of-the-ordinary experience."[15]

Offering

The offering or offertory is the gathering and presentation of alms. When Holy Communion is celebrated, the offertory also includes the presentation of bread and wine in preparation for the Great Thanksgiving, which it initiates. In order to show that these gifts come from the assembly, it is best for these gifts to be put in place by those who gather the alms and make bread and wine, or by an assisting minister representing the assembly, and not by the pastor. These people might even remain at the altar and lead the offertory prayer and assist in distributing the bread and wine at communion. The offering should help people understand themselves as giving to Christ in faith and gratitude for all Christ has done for them. At its best, the offering is a way of experiencing God's grace, just as hymns, prayers, Scripture readings, and sermons are.

Whenever I preach and lead worship as a visiting pastor, I ask my host if there is anything special, unique, or particular about the service. "No," my host usually says, "we do it like everyone else." This response is an unmistakable sign that, sometime during worship, I will be surprised and do something wrong, and someone will be upset. More often than not, that time is the offering. I will elevate the offering plates too high, too low, or not at all. I will not be told where I am supposed to be when the acolytes bring the plates to the altar—or I will be in their way. I will put the money where it does not belong. Perhaps this is why, today, many church leaders ask, "What does the language we use to define and describe the offering, the manner in which we gather and present it, and even where it occurs in the worship service, communicate about God, God's people, and the things we give?"

Reflecting on this question leads some churches to make subtle changes in the offering. For example, I was genuinely surprised when I examined my denomination's newest worship book (hymnal) and perceived that my church had made the offering "smaller." In *Lutheran Book of Worship*, the denomination's previous worship book, the presentation of the gifts of money or gifts in kind was said to have "liturgical significance," because the "gifts symbolize the 'reasonable service' (Romans 12:1) of our Christian lives offered in response to God's grace in Christ."[16] The gifts of money and the bread and wine for the Lord's Supper were brought forward by members of the congregation and were received by assisting ministers, making clear that these gifts came from the people. They were then symbolically presented to God. "After raising it slightly in a gesture of offering," the rubrics direct, "the alms basin may be removed to the credence [table]."[17] Offertories—musical settings sung by the choir—appointed for each Sunday and festival, classical choral offertories, or the congregation singing one of the general offertories provided in the worship book accompanied the presentation of the gifts. The offering concluded with an offertory or dedicatory prayer.

Jonathan Linman, adjunct professor of ascetical theology at General Theological Seminary in New York City, helps us understand the offering's liturgical significance. Dr. Linman suggests that gathering and presenting gifts in worship is our time in the liturgy to be Martha. Recalling Jesus's visit to the home of Mary and Martha (Luke 10:38–42), when Martha busied herself about the house so that she might be hospitable to Jesus, Linman calls the offering "a busy time, with seemingly competing activities, a choir singing an anthem while ushers collect money, and assisting ministers occupy themselves preparing the table."[18] When the table is ready, we return to a more contemplative mode of prayer in the spirit of Mary, as we gather around Jesus's feet, as it were, in the meal. For now, we excitedly offer ourselves to Jesus in the spirit of Martha. "All of this activity—the gathering and presentation of gifts, the musical offering, the table preparation—together constitutes a singular offering in keeping with the apostle Paul's exhortation: 'I appeal to you therefore, brothers and sisters, by the mercies of God, to present your bodies as a living sacrifice, holy and acceptable to God, which is your spiritual worship' (Romans 12:1)."[19]

In *Evangelical Lutheran Worship*, my denomination's new hymnal, the offering is described in functional rather than liturgical or theological terms. The offering is "primarily practical: collecting material goods for the mission of the church (including the care of those in need)."[20] In an effort to replace rubrics as "regulations" with "proposals and discussions for local thinking about good practice,"[21] choral music, instrumental music, and congregational singing accompanying the offering, as well as the offering prayer, are now options from which worship planners can choose—or eliminate—as they construct an offering rite. The bread and wine for communion are placed on the table; the money and material goods are placed on a side table or nearby. No mention is made of raising the alms basin slightly in a gesture of offering. Instead, the rubrics advise, "Actions and accompanying words and music that emphasize a humble and grateful response to all God's gifts will help avoid any suggestion of transaction or exchange."[22]

The Sunday Assembly, an accompanying leader guide that provides historical, theological, and practical reflections on the service of Holy Communion and the Service of the Word, suggests making the offering even smaller. The commentary changes the name from *offering*—something we bring before God—to the more functional *collection* and explains that this collection is taken prior to Holy Communion, not because the presentation of the gifts has liturgical significance but because it came to be associated with going to communion. "If God so graciously feeds us, in word and sacrament, we in response should turn toward the needs of our neighbor. We have prayed in faith for those needs. Now we share something of what we have. This is a time in which the good things of the earth, the resources God has made for the life of all, are celebrated, set out, and shared."[23] The commentary then suggests connecting the offering with going in mission to serve the poor rather than offering to God and going to communion. The commentary suggests, "Another option might be to take such a collection after we have gone to communion and as we leave the church, in the place [in the worship service] indicated in Justin Martyr's second-century report."[24] The point is that "we think carefully about how we might counter the possibility for misperception of the role of the collection. Placed here [before communion] and called an offering, this action might seem to some as if first we give payment to God and then we receive the communion."[25]

Making the offering smaller is not new. In the eighteenth and nineteenth centuries, very few Protestant churches in North America took up a regular offering as part of weekly worship. Those that did usually made special collections for a particular cause—foreign missions, home missions, or the printing of Bibles—and in those instances offerings were an on-the-spot response to the pitch made for the cause. During the closing years of the nineteenth century, the institution of the offering was rediscovered and enlarged in the life of American churches and afforded a central place in the liturgical practice of most congregations. By the 1890s, the offering was everywhere becoming a weekly ritual whereby parishioners would "present their tithes and offerings" to the Lord. The ritual of voluntarily offering up money to support the church and its benevolent activities was accompanied by prayer, procession, presentation, and singing the doxology in recognition that it was God from whom all blessings flowed. The offering ritual was usually bracketed by an admonition to "freely give as ye have freely received" and a dedicatory prayer following the doxology in which the gifts were dedicated to God. What the Reformers tried to purge—the idea that human beings independently possessed anything they could offer God—was restored to a central place of significance.[26]

Liturgical theologian Gordon W. Lathrop finds it surprising that, although Christian worship does not include elements of actual sacrifice—processing the victim, slaying animals as part of the service, using a sacred knife or bloody stone, and giving God something to eat—we use sacrificial language to describe Christian worship.[27] We call the communion table an *altar* and the collection an *offering*. Some Christian traditions call the ordained *priests*. Lathrop fears that we may "understand our giving as establishing a *do ut des* ('I give so that you should give') obligation for God to give us good things in return."[28] He acknowledges, if our use of the word *offering* leads to worship and moral living that reflects and celebrates "the all-sufficient gift of Christ rather than in any sense adding to it,"[29] this language can be and has been used to communicate the gospel. Yet, Lathrop wants us to be clear that Christians do not offer anything to God. Instead, we give thanks over all that we set out before ourselves to eat and, rather than offering food to the gods, we offer food to the poor. Therefore, Lathrop would have the church eliminate all hints of transaction by calling the offering *collection* and relocating the collection until after we receive communion and are leaving the church.

William Seth Adams, an Anglican liturgical scholar, observes, "Even though Gordon Lathrop is obviously right in saying that we Christians do not literally make sacrifice, given talk of altars and given that we carry 'gifts' to them, there is something of the 'look' of a sacrificial event, even to those for whom the theological idea of sacrifice would be unattractive."[30] Adams reflects, "In the form of our alms and bread and wine carried through the congregation as is our custom, the people standing, and in the metaphorical sense on which we have relied earlier, we can 'see' *ourselves* being carried to a place of sacrifice, there to be made holy, surrendered, there to pass over into God's own possession. And in that this is so for ourselves, we can 'see' that it is so also for all of creation. What a compelling moment this might be, when rightly 'seen,' a moment compelling thanksgiving and engagement in the life of the world."[31]

Mark P. Bangert, professor emeritus of worship at Lutheran School of Theology at Chicago, rightly observes, "Money gifts, as well as talents, time, and possessions ritually connected to bread and wine [of communion] challenge us to rethink 'stuff,' to reconsider our habits of accumulation, to embrace creation as sustaining gift, and to *spend* for the lives of humans, animals, and plants." Bangert declares, "Only then can we sing rightfully those happy words: 'Heaven and earth are full of your glory.'"[32] As I indicated in chapter 4, Charles Campbell considers the offering and giving money away a faith practice by which Christians publicly resist the power of mammon and embody their loyalty to the living God.

I genuinely appreciate the careful and creative theological reflection on what the church says and does by the way it gathers money and presents bread and wine during worship. I am, however, concerned that making the offering smaller will also lead to misinterpretation. For example, making the offering smaller by placing the bread and wine on the altar table prior to the service, rather than bringing them forward, may lend the bread and wine a lofty, even magical, quality. Not bringing the money forward may reinforce a dichotomy between the sacredness of worship and the secular business of money. Changing the offering's place in the service might also create confusion. While paying prior to receiving a meal is the practice when eating fast-food, giving money after we have eaten and as we are leaving is the pattern in most other restaurants. Taking a collection after communion as we are leaving the church may therefore suggest that we must pay for the communion we received, as we do when we go out to eat.

If the point is to avoid any hint of transaction, of needing to pay God either so we can receive or because we have received grace, the preacher might directly or indirectly make this point about the offering in the sermon by preaching the gospel, particularly on Consecration Sunday. The congregation might also follow the example of Ambrose, the fourth-century bishop of Milan, and many seeker-oriented congregations today. Ambrose prohibited those who might misperceive or misinterpret the offering from participating in it.[33] Ambrose reports that, though those baptized at the Easter Vigil received communion at that worship service, they were not permitted to participate in the people's offering of bread and wine before the octave of Easter. Recalling the eight days of the Jewish period for purification, Ambrose gives as the reason for this exclusion the fact that this ceremony can be performed only by people who know its meaning and have become established as Christians. Ambrose's assertion is especially striking, since he gives no instruction on baptism, the Eucharist, and the Lord's Prayer until *after* those preparing for baptism experienced these rites for the first time when they are baptized, have prayed the Lord's Prayer, and have received Holy Communion at the Easter Vigil. In fact, until their baptism, those to be baptized were dismissed after the liturgy of the Word to preserve the secrecy of the Eucharist. The celebration of the Eucharist at the Easter Vigil was not only the first time the newly baptized received communion; it was also their first time observing the celebration of the Eucharist, and teaching came after participation.[34] Yet, the newly baptized could not participate in the offering until they had been taught its meaning. This is completely opposite of presenting offering envelopes to candidates for confirmation before they are confirmed.

Commenting on Ambrose excluding the newly baptized from participating in the offering while including them in baptism and the Lord's Supper, liturgical scholar Edward Yarnold, SJ, asserts, "It is hard to imagine why the neophytes [newly baptized] who had been initiated into many more precious mysteries should be debarred from this far more commonplace rite."[35] Yarnold rightfully asks, "Why does participation in the offertory require more careful preparation than communion?"[36] Yarnold answers his own question when he asserts "the Fathers frequently saw the Offertory as the congregation's offering of themselves."[37] Prohibiting the newly baptized from participating in the offering until after the octave of Easter is in keeping with Ambrose's understanding of both baptism and communion as God's actions. The role of the newly baptized throughout the Easter Vigil is to receive God's grace. Those baptized and taking communion do not need to understand what is happening to them in order to receive it. On the other hand, the offering is a response to God's grace: it is the ritual expression by which the faithful offer themselves to God. A sincere response requires understanding, which the newly baptized will receive through instruction from the bishop during the week following Easter. It is, therefore, appropriate for them to wait to participate in the offering until the Sunday after Easter. If the church is concerned that people might misunderstand the offering as somehow purchasing God's grace or favor, might we prohibit those who do not understand the offering as our freely giving ourselves in grateful response for all that God graciously gives us from participating in it?

Edward J. Kilmartin, SJ, writes, "The highest virtue and truly perfect act of love consists in the complete surrender to God of one's whole being and in placing one's possessions at [God's] disposal."[38] I find myself wondering what we can do to communicate this truth by the way we celebrate the collection or offering, and how we might preach on this liturgical act as an experience of grace. How might we explore different ways of collecting and receiving money, bread, and wine in worship that embody and celebrate giving in response to the gospel?

In answering this question, I find myself looking to "bigger" ways of giving our money, our possessions, and ourselves to God in worship. For example, compare the offering in your congregation to a thanksgiving service in the Bulawayo parish in Zimbabwe. People without money offered what they had—a bag of grain, two men's suits, and a rooster. "It was amazing!" an American visitor observed. "This man walked through the sanctuary with a screeching rooster. It was the hot item." The congregation auctioned off what people offered to provide for the ministry of the church. A Lutheran bishop shared with me that, when he was in Tanzania, someone offered a cow, which was to be entrusted to an evangelist. This man placed the cow in the bishop's care so that the cow would provide the evangelist milk to sustain him as he traveled sharing the gospel. Both American visitors were clear that, when these Christians offered their gifts, they were not transacting with God; they were gratefully giving of themselves as a response to and participation in the gospel.

What can we do to make the offering bigger? Even as I ask the question, the idea of making the offering bigger makes me nervous. I wholeheartedly agree with Adams that our attitude when offering substantial things and ourselves needs to be one of serious and sincere modesty, even as we give joyfully. Adams writes, "Though unintended by Christians in the developed west, there is arrogance about our offering processions that can be seen with clarity by those who view our parades of food and money from a place of hunger and want. Our offering is made hypocritical if what we give is exhausted by our own use, our own maintenance and continuance of our own well-being. Our action of offering is made less hypocritical if what we give is 'sacrificed' for the good of the world, used *imitatio Christi,* in the imitation of One who saved others but could not save himself."[39] Taking Adams's caution most seriously, I continue to ask how we might make the offering bigger. The preachers and congregational leaders I ask offer suggestions such as these:

- Invite people to bring both money and food gifts and place them in large baskets at the altar-table. Money offerings are literally put into perspective by the much larger food items. The bills, coins, and checks slip in and are almost swallowed up among the cans of tuna fish, the bags of rice, and the cans of soup. A worshiper wrote, "That moment stuck with me—seeing my money physically connected to food for the hungry. And of course the unusual procession forward for all of us to bring our gifts."

- Create a space near the credence table for the offering baskets, where a congregation might commission a modest-sized but beautifully crafted mosaic, icon, or painting of Christ feeding the multitudes, or Christ the healer, or the peaceable kingdom—a visible weekly connection between the offerings and the promised reign of God, and a reminder that God heals the world and we do not heal the world on our own.

- Designate an extra part of benevolence giving to local ministries, with one selected for each liturgical season. Sometime
  early in the season, invite a representative from that ministry to
  worship with the congregation and share a brief word of greet-
  ing and interpretation of their mission—and the congregation's
  connection to it.
- Carry the offerings out—especially the food offerings—as part
  of the recessional, and take them directly to be bagged in the
  fellowship hall, or straight to a shelter or social ministry site.
  While congregations must take care so that the sending of the
  collection or offering does not become a self-congratulatory pa-
  rade, we bring food to the hungry in the same way that we bring
  communion to the homebound.
- On a particular Sunday, take a *collection* for a special project.
  The following Sunday, surprise the congregation with the news
  that the collection had been taken, counted, and then divided
  up, somewhat randomly, and distributed back to the congregational households via their mailboxes. Each household receives
  a gift from the church in an amount ranging from twenty to a
  few hundred dollars. Their job, as a household or family unit, is
  to decide how best to spend that money in service of the coming
  reign of God. They can keep it for themselves, give it to a charity
  organization, buy supplies for a homeless shelter, or give it to
  a microloan operation. Then, over the next weeks and months
  in worship, at the time for the offering, particular households
  come forward, and as the offering is received by the whole congregation, the members of the one household give testimony of
  what they did with their money and why.
- Frame the offering as a form of praise. The members of one congregation dance and sing in procession as they bring their offering to the front of the nave.

Regardless of how we might reimagine or reinterpret the collection in
worship, I am convinced God's people attach great significance to the
offering. I have also learned that there is no one right way to do it. The
question, then, is how, in your congregation, people can give and the
church can receive money in a way that is in keeping with and a faith-

ful response to God's gracious and unconditional love in Jesus Christ. Once congregations determine how to best do the offering, perhaps the remaining pieces of the stewardship campaign will fall into place.

AS YOU PREPARE YOUR SERMON . . .

- What does your congregation's annual stewardship campaign look like? How long has your congregation been doing it the same way? What might you do differently this year?

- How do children and adults in your congregation learn what the Bible teaches about money and giving? What are you intentionally and unintentionally teaching?

- Does your congregation use pledge or estimate of giving cards? Why or why not?

- Is placing money in an offering envelope different from paying a bill? How?

- Which of the components of a stewardship campaign discussed in this chapter are you most eager for your congregation to try? Which one gives you the most anxiety? Why?

- What does the offering or collection in worship mean to you? How does the way your congregation conducts the offering strengthen and challenge your faith? How might your congregation collect, present, and receive the money, bread, and wine differently?

Afterword

BEFORE YOU BEGIN that stewardship sermon, sit back, take a breath, read the following passage aloud several times, and hear the word of God.

> When you have come into the land that the LORD your God is giving you as an inheritance to possess, and you possess it, and settle in it, you shall take some of the first of all the fruit of the ground, which you harvest from the land that the LORD your God is giving you, and you shall put it in a basket and go to the place that the LORD your God will choose as a dwelling for his name. You shall go to the priest who is in office at that time, and say to him, "Today I declare to the LORD your God that I have come into the land that the LORD swore to our ancestors to give us." When the priest takes the basket from your hand and sets it down before the altar of the LORD your God, you shall make this response before the LORD your God: "A wandering Aramean was my ancestor; he went down into Egypt and lived there as an alien, few in number, and there he became a great nation, mighty and populous. When the Egyptians treated us harshly and afflicted us, by imposing hard labor on us, we cried to the LORD, the God of our ancestors; the LORD heard our voice and saw our affliction, our toil, and our oppression. The LORD brought us out of Egypt with a mighty hand and an outstretched arm, with a terrifying display of power, and with signs and wonders; and he brought us into this place and gave us this land, a land flowing with milk and honey. So now I bring the first of the fruit of the

ground that you, O LORD, have given me." You shall set it down before
the LORD your God and bow down before the LORD your God. Then
you, together with the Levites and the aliens who reside among you,
shall celebrate with all the bounty that the LORD your God has given to
you and to your house.

DEUTERONOMY 26:1–11

Today, many who write about and teach Christian liturgy turn to Luke's
account of the road to Emmaus (Luke 24:13–33) as a model of the
church's worship. Like the disciples traveling to Emmaus, worshipers
gather with Jesus, hear the Word spoken, receive the bread broken, and
are sent in joy with good news of resurrection. In the same way that
we imagine ourselves as Cleopas and his companion walking the road
to Emmaus, so we can claim our identity as spiritual descendants of
that "wandering Aramean." When we do, we find in Deuteronomy 26 a
model of giving as an act of worship—an offering—in gratitude to the
God who lovingly and graciously delivered us in Jesus Christ.

Like the offering that we give in worship, Deuteronomy 26 describes
a liturgical act of gratitude for God's particular grace that ends in mission—a celebration that includes "the aliens who reside among you."
Deuteronomy reminds us that making the offering is a way that we, as
worshipers, remember who we were—wandering Arameans like Jacob,
with nothing to commend us. We remember that God made the first
move. Hearing our cries and seeing our affliction, God rescued us from
oppression and brought us on a journey through life's wilderness. Along
the way, God always remained faithful to us. We remember that we
have entered into God's promises. By giving first fruits and reciting a
story of deliverance, we confess God's faithfulness as our life's foundation, because God's gracious providing leads us to gratefully claim this
story of deliverance as our own.

Of course, for us to understand these verses from Deuteronomy as
a model of giving in response to the gospel, we need to regard "the land
that the LORD your God is giving you, . . . the land that the LORD swore to
our ancestors to give us, . . . a land flowing with milk and honey" meta-
phorically, as the early church did. Just as God brought Israel through
the sea to the land of promise, so in baptism Christ brings us through
the water to the promised land of the forgiveness of sins, union with
Christ, a share in the reign of God, and life everlasting. Cyril of Jerusalem speaks of baptism as entering the promised land this way:

Of old Moses was sent into Egypt by God, but in our era Christ is sent
into the world by the Father. As Moses was appointed to lead his af-
flicted people from Egypt, so Christ came to deliver the people of the
world who were overcome by sin. As the blood of the lamb served to
avert the destroyer, so the blood of Jesus Christ, the blameless lamb,
had the effect of routing demons. That tyrant of old pursued the an-
cient Jewish people as far as the sea, and here and now the devil, bold
and shameless, the source of all evil, followed you up to the waters of
salvation. Pharaoh was submerged in the sea, and the devil disappears
in the waters of salvation.[1]

Passing through the waters of baptism, we arrive safely in the "land flowing with milk and honey" that God promised and through Christ gives
to us. Understanding baptism in this way, it is not surprising that the
"Apostolic Tradition," a so-called church order attributed to Hippolytus
of Rome, states that, when the newly baptized received the Eucharist
for the first time at the Easter Vigil during which they were baptized,
they partook of a two special cups in addition to the cup of wine. One
cup contained water and the other cup contained a mixture of milk and
honey—a gustatory symbol of Christ's flesh as the promised land flowing with milk and honey into which they had finally entered through
baptismal waters. Tertullian mentions this ceremony early in the third
century, and it was still practiced in Rome in the sixth century.[2] Heard
in this way, Deuteronomy provides a model of how to faithfully respond to God when we have passed through the waters of baptism and
entered into the promised land flowing with milk and honey that is our
inheritance because we belong to Christ.

As those who have come into the promised land that is Christ, who
possess God's promises, and who are settling into a life of discipleship
empowered by the Spirit, we bring some of the first fruits of our lives
and our possessions to our church, where we are so aware of God's
presence that we are tempted to think of it as God's dwelling place.
Here our first fruits are collected and brought to the altar, from where
they are used for the work of the gospel. Our first fruits are something
we give to God before anything else. They are our best. They are something we personally select.

Deuteronomy instructs putting some of the first fruit of the ground
in a basket. Commentators contend that the basket suggests that people brought grapes as well as grain. As Christians, we can understand

bringing grapes and grain as a sign that God will use everything we bring to further God's own work in the world, as surely as the grapes and grain we bring becomes Eucharist. This is so because, when we pray and proclaim with thanksgiving over bread and wine, Christ's presence empowers us to use everything we are and everything we have to participate in Christ's own work of bringing love, justice, and life to the world.

As you prepare the stewardship sermon, you might ask yourself what confession of faith you would have your people make as they bring first fruits—estimate of giving cards, offering envelopes, canned goods, or their time and talents—to Christ's altar. How would you have your people speak of God delivering them from bondage, guiding them through the wilderness, and bringing them to the land of promise? Looking through the epistles—Romans 5:8, Ephesians 2:3, 2 Thessalonians 3:3, and Romans 8:38–39—I found myself answering the question this way:

> When I was far off, Christ came near to me. When I was lost in sin, Christ died for me. As I make my way in this world, Christ remains faithful to me. And nothing, not even death, can separate me from Christ's love. And so I bring the first of the fruits of all that God has entrusted to me as a token of my gratitude and a pledge to use everything God gives me to proclaim Christ's love and to participate in Christ's own work in the world.

What confession of faith would you have your people make as they bring first fruits—estimate of giving cards, offering envelopes, canned goods, or their time and talents—to Christ's altar? The grace in asking this question is that, when you answer it, you will know what to preach—and you will find yourself eager to preach it.

May God bless you and keep you as you prepare your sermon. May God bring you joy in proclaiming the good news of giving to the church in response to the gospel.

Money and Giving in the Revised Common Lectionary

Year A

Second Sunday after Christmas

Jeremiah 31:7–14. God will satisfy us with God's bounty.
Ephesians 1:3–14. In Christ, God lavishes on us the riches of grace.

Second Sunday after Epiphany

1 Corinthians 1:1–9. Paul celebrates God, who enriched the Corinthians in every way. As they wait for the revealing of Jesus, they lack no spiritual gift.

Third Sunday after Epiphany

Micah 6:1–8. God does not require us to give perfect gifts, make extravagant offerings, or sever our most precious relationships. Instead, God requires us simply to do justice, love kindness, and walk humbly with God.

1 Corinthians 1:18–31. God chose the nothings in the world to reduce to nothing the somethings, so none of us can boast before God.

Matthew 5:1–12. Jesus promises blessing for the spiritually impoverished and those who spend themselves in God's service, whether or not they are materially rich or poor.

Fifth Sunday after Epiphany

Isaiah 58:1–9a [9b–12]. The fast God requires involves material and financial support of people in need.

Sixth Sunday after Epiphany

Deuteronomy 30:15–20. After giving us what we need to live, God guides us toward a life worth living.

1 Corinthians 3:1–9. God gives wages according to our labor, not according to our results.

Matthew 5:21–37. Jesus is more eager for us to make peace with each other than for us to make offerings to God.

Seventh Sunday after Epiphany

Leviticus 19:1–2, 9–18. Holy living involves, among other things, leaving the edges and leftovers of what is ours for the poor, not stealing or defrauding, not delaying payment of workers, not having courts partial to poor or rich, and not profiting by the blood of our neighbors.

Matthew 5:38–48. Jesus teaches us how to be perfect as God is perfect, giving our cloak to anyone who sues for only our coat and giving to anyone who begs or asks to borrow.

Eighth Sunday after Epiphany

Isaiah 49:8–16a. Like a woman nursing her child, God will not forget to feed us.

1 Corinthians 4:1–5. God, rather than human courts, judges whether we are trustworthy stewards.

Matthew 6:24–34. Jesus frees us from worrying about money and the things we need, so we can serve only God and strive first for God's kingdom.

Ash Wednesday

Isaiah 58:1–12. The fast God requires involves material and financial support of people in need.

Matthew 6:1–6, 16–21. Jesus warns that we will receive no reward when we donate money in order to receive praise, and he invites us to consider where we invest because it reveals where our hearts truly are. Or, Jesus invites us to train our hearts by putting our treasure where we want our hearts to be.

First Sunday in Lent

Romans 5:12–19. Grace abounds and righteousness is freely given in Jesus Christ.

Matthew 4:1–11. Jesus refuses to give us dead bread but instead gives us only the truly living bread of his own self.

Second Sunday in Lent

Romans 4:1–5, 13–17. What we would rather earn, Jesus gives for free.

Second Sunday of Easter

1 Peter 1:3–9. As we suffer, God makes our faith genuine and more precious than gold.

Third Sunday of Easter

1 Peter 1:17–23. We were ransomed with the precious and eternal blood of Christ, not with temporary things like silver or gold.

Fourth Sunday of Easter

Acts 2:42–47. Christ's resurrection renewed the life of the church, awakening devotion to worship, fellowship, and study, inspiring awe-filled expectation and action, and forming a community of believers who shared all things in common, sold their possessions, gave the proceeds to all as had need. Glad and generous also with their hearts, their time, their praise to God, the church's generosity begot generosity in others, who gave in return their goodwill and themselves.

1 Peter 2:19–25. We gain when we, like Christ, endure unjust suffering for others' sake.

Fifth Sunday of Easter

1 Peter 2:2–10. Jesus is a living, precious stone.

Vigil of Pentecost

Exodus 19:1–9. We are God's treasured possessions, not our treasure or our possessions.

Romans 8:14–17, 22–27. The Spirit confirms the promise within us: On the other side of our suffering, we, as children and heirs of God, will receive our inheritance.

Sunday between May 24 and 28 inclusive

Isaiah 49:8–16a. Like a woman nursing her child, God will not forget to feed us.

1 Corinthians 4:1–5. God judges whether we are trustworthy stewards, not human courts.

Matthew 6:24–34. Jesus frees us from worrying about money and the things we need, so we can serve God alone and strive first for God's kingdom.

Sunday between June 5 and 11 inclusive

Hosea 5:15—6:6. God desires steadfast love, not sacrifice.

Romans 4:13–25. We are heirs by God's grace, not by our adherence to the law.

Sunday between June 12 and 18 inclusive

Exodus 19:2–8a. We are God's treasured possessions, not our treasure or our possessions.

Matthew 9:35—10:8 [9–23]. God provides for God's empty-handed messengers through the hospitality of strangers.

Sunday between June 19 and 25 inclusive

Matthew 10:24–39. Jesus values us much more than many pennies.

Sunday between June 26 and July 2

Romans 6:12–23. The wages of sin is death, but the free gift of God is eternal life in Christ Jesus our Lord.

Matthew 10:40–42. God rewards everyone who welcomes God's people or who shares as little as a glass of water with the thirsty.

Sunday between July 17 and 23 inclusive

Romans 8:12–25. The Spirit confirms the promise within us: On the other side of our suffering, we, as children and heirs of God, will receive our inheritance.

Sunday between July 24 and 30 inclusive

1 Kings 3:5–12. God delights to give Solomon wisdom because he did not ask, among other things, for riches. Then God gives riches and more besides.

Matthew 13:31–33, 44–52. The kingdom of heaven is more valuable than everything we own put together.

Sunday between July 31 and August 6 inclusive

Isaiah 55:1–5. We spend our money on cheap knockoffs of what is truly satisfying and nourishing, but God gives away the real thing for free.

Matthew 14:13–21. Jesus multiplies our gifts.

Sunday between August 14 and 20 inclusive

Isaiah 56:1, 6–8. God accepts the offerings of all peoples.

Genesis 45:1–15 (semicontinuous). Finding God's grace hidden even within the evil in his life, Joseph gives with abundant generosity forgiveness as well as material and financial support for his wayward brothers.

Romans 11:1–2a, 29–32. God's gifts are irrevocable.

Sunday between August 21 and 27 inclusive

Exodus 1:8—2:10 (semicontinuous). God sides with abused workers.

Sunday between August 28 and September 3 inclusive

Exodus 3:1–5 (semicontinuous). God frees slaves.

Romans 12:9–21. Paul links genuine love with contributing to the needs of the saints and encourages us to feed and give drink to hungry and thirsty enemies.

Matthew 16:21–28. We cannot buy back our lives, but Jesus did, so we can spend them in following Jesus.

Sunday between September 4 and 10 inclusive

Romans 13:8–14. Renewed by the grace of owing nothing to God, we may live that same grace in our human relationships, owing nothing to anyone.

Sunday between September 11 and 17 inclusive

Genesis 50:15–21. God's gracious presence in hardship makes us people who provide materially and financially for those who have hurt us.

Matthew 18:21–35. In the kingdom of heaven, there is forgiveness of debts. Period.

Sunday between September 18 and 24 inclusive

Exodus 16:2–15 (semicontinuous). God satisfies our need.

Matthew 20:1–16. God hires those no one else hires and offers the daily wage to all workers.

Sunday between September 25 and October 1 inclusive

Philippians 2:1–13. Even the slightest comfort from Jesus and the Spirit's smallest movements lead us to look to others' interests instead of our own, financial and otherwise.

Sunday between October 2 and 8 inclusive

Isaiah 5:1–7. God intends us to be a fruitful and generous vineyard, and God will never give up on us, because God loves us.

Philippians 3:4b–14. Paul willingly suffered every loss for the surpassing gain of life in Jesus Christ.

Matthew 21:33–46. Jesus gave his life to make the ungenerous generous.

Sunday between October 9 and 15 inclusive

Isaiah 25:1–9. God, refuge for the poor, offers a rich feast for all peoples.

Sunday between October 16 and 22 inclusive

Isaiah 45:1–7. God gives us the treasures of darkness and the riches hidden in secret places.

Matthew 22:15–22. Jesus invites us to give to Caesar what is Caesar's and to God what is God's.

Sunday between October 23 and 29 inclusive

Leviticus 19:1–2, 15–18. Holy living involves, among other things, leaving the edges and leftovers of what is ours for the poor, not stealing or defrauding, not delaying payment of workers, not having courts partial to poor or rich, and not profiting by the blood of our neighbors.

Sunday between October 30 and November 5 inclusive

Micah 3:5–12. God frees God's Word, bringing down prophets who soothe the well-fed while attacking the hungry, and ruining rulers, priests, and prophets who demand bribes and expect payment.

Sunday between November 6 and 12 inclusive

Amos 5:18–24. God refuses our offerings, along with our worship and song, when we dam up justice and righteousness.

Sunday between November 13 and 19 inclusive

Zephaniah 1:7, 12–18. Neither our silver nor our gold nor any of our possessions can save us from God's anger at our complacency.

Matthew 25:14–30. Jesus invites us to invest for the sake of God's kingdom the money God has entrusted to us.

Year B

Fourth Sunday in Advent

2 Samuel 7:1–11, 16. God makes a house for us, not us a house for God.

First Sunday after Christmas

Galatians 4:4–7. Jesus made us children of God, heirs not slaves.

Second Sunday after Christmas

Jeremiah 31:7–14. God will satisfy us with God's bounty.
Ephesians 1:3–14. In Christ, God lavishes on us the riches of grace.

Second Sunday after Epiphany

1 Samuel 3:1–10 [11–20]. Our offering cannot cancel sin, but Jesus's did.

1 Corinthians 6:12–20. Jesus bought us with the price of his body, so we may use our bodies to glorify God.

Third Sunday after Epiphany

1 Corinthians 7:29–31. Jesus raises us to live as though we have no possessions.

Mark 1:14–20. Whatever we do for a living, Jesus lets us work for him.

Fifth Sunday after Epiphany

1 Corinthians 9:16–23. Our reward for serving God is offering the things of God for free.

Sixth Sunday after Epiphany

2 Kings 5:1–15. God's healing is both more free and more expensive than we budgeted.

1 Corinthians 9:24–27. Jesus frees us to strive for an imperishable prize.

Seventh Sunday after Epiphany

Isaiah 43:18–25. Because we have wearied of giving to God, God will do a new thing. God will give more.

Ash Wednesday

Isaiah 58:1–12. The fast God requires involves material and financial support of people in need.

Matthew 6:1–6, 16–21. Jesus warns that we will receive no reward when we donate money in order to receive praise, and he invites us to consider where we invest because it reveals where our hearts truly are. Or, Jesus invites us to train our hearts by putting our treasure where we want our hearts to be.

Second Sunday in Lent

Mark 8:31–38. We cannot buy back our lives, but Jesus did, so we can spend them in following Jesus.

Third Sunday in Lent

John 2:13–22. Jesus, the lamb of God, gave his life so our zeal for money would become zeal for God.

Fourth Sunday in Lent

Ephesians 2:1–10. Christ raised us to dwell in the immeasurable riches of God's grace.

Second Sunday of Easter

Acts 4:32–35. After Christ has shared death and new life with us, what money and possessions can we withhold from each other?

Fourth Sunday of Easter

1 John 3:16–24. God's abiding love releases us from our money and material things, so we can use them to help brothers and sisters in need.

John 10:11–18. Jesus does what no others would do for us, even if we paid them, because Jesus loves us.

Fifth Sunday of Easter

Acts 8:26–40. What will the Holy Spirit do to the budget when the treasurer discovers the good news about Jesus in the prophets?

Vigil of Pentecost

Exodus 19:1–9. We are God's treasured possessions, not our treasure or our possessions.

Romans 8:14–17, 22–27. The Spirit confirms the promise within us: On the other side of our suffering, we, as children and heirs of God, will receive our inheritance.

Sunday between May 29 and June 4 inclusive

Deuteronomy 5:12–15. God gives us a day absent of earning a paycheck, so we can learn what it means to be free.

Mark 2:23—3:6. Jesus stands up for the ones who must work to eat on the day everybody else gets to rest.

Sunday between June 5 and 11 inclusive

1 Samuel 8:4–11 [12–15] 16–20; [11:14–15] (semicontinuous). Samuel elaborates God's warning to Israel about their desire for a king, including that a king will take one-tenth of their grain, grapes, and flocks and the best of their cattle and donkeys.

Sunday between June 19 and 25 inclusive

2 Corinthians 6:1–13. God lavishes grace on us through servants of God who though poor make us rich and while having nothing possess everything.

Sunday between June 26 and July 2

2 Corinthians 8:7–15. Paul encourages us to excel in giving as we already excel in faith, speech, knowledge, and eagerness. Be as generous as you are beloved, he says. Then Paul reminds us that the One who became poor to make us rich judges our giving with equal generosity: according to what we have, not according to what we do not have; according to how fairly we balance our abundance with others' need, not according to how poor we make ourselves.

Sunday between July 3 and 9 inclusive

Mark 6:1–13. God provides for God's empty-handed messengers through the hospitality of strangers.

Sunday between July 10 and 16 inclusive

Ephesians 1:3–14. In Christ, God lavishes on us the riches of grace.

Sunday between July 17 and 23 inclusive

2 Samuel 7:1–14a (semicontinuous). God makes a house for us, not us a house for God.

Sunday between July 24 and 30 inclusive

2 Kings 4:42–44. God multiplies our gifts.

John 6:1–21. Jesus gives far more than we can pay for, satisfying us and with extra to share.

Sunday between July 31 and August 6 inclusive

Exodus 16:2–4, 9–15. God satisfies our need.

John 6:24–35. Jesus teaches the crowd he fed to work for food that endures for eternal life, not that perishes, and he promises that all who come to Jesus will never be hungry or thirsty.

Sunday between August 7 and 13 inclusive

1 Kings 19:4–8. God feeds us even when we'd rather die.

Ephesians 4:25—5:2. One of Paul's examples of what it means to imitate God and love as Christ loved us is to give up stealing and work honestly, so we can share with the needy.

John 6:35, 41–51. Jesus is the living bread from heaven, even when we don't understand or believe it.

Sunday between August 14 and 20 inclusive

1 Kings 2:10–12; 3:3–14 (semicontinuous). God delights to give Solomon wisdom because he did not ask, among other things, for riches. Then God gives riches and more besides.

Sunday between August 28 and September 3 inclusive

James 1:17–27. Every generous act of giving is itself a gift given by God.

Sunday between September 4 and 10 inclusive

Proverbs 22:1–2, 8–9, 22–23 (semicontinuous). A handful of wise sayings about rich and poor, generosity and justice reveal God's special concern for the poor and the generous.

James 2:1–10 [10–13] 14–17. Because God chose the poor to be rich in faith, James encourages us not to favor people who can give us money, possessions, or status. Instead, he invites us to a living, life-giving faith that supplies for the bodily needs of others.

Mark 7:24–37. Jesus wastes for us.

Sunday between September *11* and *17* inclusive

Mark 8:27–38. We cannot buy back our lives, but Jesus did, so we can spend them in following Jesus.

Sunday between September *25* and October *1* inclusive

Esther 7:1–6, 9–10; 9:20–22 (semicontinuous). The day of celebration includes sending presents to the poor.

Sunday between October *9* and *15* inclusive

Amos 5:6–7, 10–15. Amos tells the truth: seizing grain from the poor to satisfy their debt is evil, as is bribery, which effectively sidelines the needy in the public square. Turning away from these practices leads back to God, to justice, and to life.

Mark 10:17–31. To a man who has everything, including a good reputation, Jesus offers the only thing worth having: a chance to give it all away for the sake of the poor and become an unencumbered follower of Jesus and a full inheritor of eternal life.

Sunday between October *30* and November *5* inclusive

Deuteronomy 6:1–9. Moses promises that wholehearted faithfulness to the One who freed us leads to true prosperity.

Ruth 1:1–18 (semi-continuous). Even in a foreign land, God is known to care for and feed God's people.

Sunday between November *6* and *12* inclusive

1 Kings 17:8–16. Sharing God's message and ministry of life, Elijah did not hesitate to seek support even from a destitute widow, whom God empowered to be generous.

Mark 12:38–44. Incensed by religious leaders' hypocrisy and corruption and unmoved by large donations by the rich, Jesus sees and celebrates a poor widow's greatest gift in the two smallest coins.

Sunday between November 13 and 19 inclusive

Hebrews 10:11–14 [15–18] 19–25. We are saved by Jesus's offering, not our own.

Year C

Third Sunday in Advent

Luke 3:7–18. John the Baptist offers three examples of repentance: giving away what is in excess of need, no longer overcharging or extorting, and being satisfied with fair wages.

Fourth Sunday in Advent

Hebrews 10:5–10. We are saved by Jesus's offering, not our own.
Luke 1:39–55. Mary praises God for filling the poor and emptying the rich.

Third Sunday after Epiphany

Nehemiah 8:1–3, 5–6, 8–10. As worship ends, the people are invited to go, feast, and share portions with those who have none.

Fourth Sunday after Epiphany

1 Corinthians 13:1–13. Without love, what do we gain by giving away everything we own?

Sixth Sunday after Epiphany

Luke 6:17–26. Jesus proclaims blessing for those who have less than they need and woe for those who have more.

Seventh Sunday after Epiphany

Luke 6:27–38. Jesus describes what it means to love enemies and show mercy, including giving to all beggars, not seeking restitution from thieves and in fact giving them more than they steal, and lending, expecting nothing in return.

Ash Wednesday

Isaiah 58:1–12. The fast God requires involves material and financial support of people in need.

Matthew 6:1–6, 16–21. Jesus warns that we will receive no reward when we donate money in order to receive praise, and he invites us to consider where we invest because it reveals where our hearts truly are. Or, Jesus invites us to train our hearts by putting our treasure where we want our hearts to be.

First Sunday in Lent

Deuteronomy 26:1–11. The first fruits belong to God because they grow from God's abundant generosity.

Third Sunday in Lent

Isaiah 55:1–9. We spend our money on cheap knockoffs of what is truly satisfying and nourishing, but God gives away the real thing for free.

Fourth Sunday in Lent

Luke 15:1–3, 11b–32. No matter how we have wasted what God has given, God spends even more to welcome us home.

Sixth Sunday of Easter

Acts 16:9–15. After one sermon, Lydia, a successful businesswoman, insists Paul and Silas make use of her household and wealth for the sake of the gospel.

Seventh Sunday of Easter

Acts 16:16–34. When Paul and Silas share the freedom of the gospel, the city's business community, people, and government perceive them as a threat to their bottom line and "way of life," attacking and imprisoning them. But God sets free all the prisoners and even the city jailer, who in turn opens home and table to Paul and Silas.

Revelation 22:12–14, 16–17, 20–21. The water of life is a gift.

Vigil of Pentecost

Exodus 19:1–9. We are God's treasured possessions, not our treasure or our possessions.

Romans 8:14–17, 22–27. The Spirit confirms the promise within us: On the other side of our suffering, we, as children and heirs of God, will receive our inheritance.

Day of Pentecost

Romans 8:14–17. The Spirit confirms the promise within us: On the other side of our suffering, we, as children and heirs of God, will receive our inheritance.

Sunday between June 5 and 11 inclusive

1 Kings 17:8–16 [17–24] (semicontinuous). Sharing God's message and ministry of life, Elijah did not hesitate to seek support even from a destitute widow, whom God empowered to be generous.

Sunday between June 12 and 18 inclusive

Luke 7:36—8:3. God's extravagant generosity begets extravagant generosity.

Sunday between July 3 and 9 inclusive

Luke 10:1–11, 16–20. God provides for God's empty-handed messengers through the hospitality of strangers.

Sunday between July 10 and 16 inclusive

Deuteronomy 30:9–14. God delights in prospering us, starting with our heart and soul.

Luke 10:25–37. The Samaritan showed mercy by investing his time, attention, and money in the man's healing.

Sunday between July 17 and 23 inclusive

Amos 8:1–12 (semicontinuous). By letting us gorge ourselves on greed, God awakens our hunger for God. (See also "Year C, Sunday between September 18 and 24 inclusive.")

Sunday between July 24 and 30 inclusive

Luke 11:1–13. God is a giver who wants to be bothered.

Sunday between July 31 and August 6 inclusive

Luke 12:13–21. Saving us from all kinds of greed, Jesus frees us to live life rich toward God.

Sunday between August 7 and 13 inclusive

Isaiah 1:1, 10–20 (semicontinuous). God launders us, not our money.

Luke 12:32–40. Because God gives us the kingdom, we can release our frightened grip on our money and possessions.

Sunday between August 14 and 20 inclusive

Isaiah 5:1–7 (semicontinuous). God lets the vineyard thrive that yields good grapes.

Sunday between August 21 and 27 inclusive

Isaiah 58:9b–14. God satisfies and strengthens those who share food and tend to others' material needs.

Sunday between August 28 and September 3 inclusive

Jeremiah 2:4–13 (semicontinuous). To people who went after worthless things, God offers priceless living water.

Hebrews 13:1–8, 15–16. Jesus loves us more than we love money.

Luke 14:1, 7–14. Jesus invites us to a banquet we cannot repay.

Sunday between September 4 and 10 inclusive

Deuteronomy 30:15–20. After giving us what we need to live, God guides us toward a life worth living.

Philemon 1–21. No one can own us, because we belong to Christ.

Luke 14:25–33. Jesus counted then paid the cost to free us from our things.

Sunday between September 18 and 24 inclusive

Amos 8:4–7. God sees how we do business and counts who loses when we profit, and God's justice will prevail.

Luke 16:1–13. God masters the money that mastered us.

Sunday between September 25 and October 1 inclusive

Amos 6:1a, 4–7. Exile is God's way of healing those made numb by financial security.

Jeremiah 32:1–3a, 6–15 (semicontinuous). God invests where we will not.

1 Timothy 6:6–9. Jesus raises maimed money lovers to life: life contented, generous, and joyful.

Luke 16:19–31. God gives Lazarus the rest of our lives. God turns the tables of rich and poor.

Sunday between October 2 and 8 inclusive

2 Timothy 1:1–14. God gives true treasure: faith.

Sunday between October 9 and 15 inclusive

Jeremiah 29:1, 4–7 (semicontinuous). God weaves our welfare with the welfare of our neighbors.

Luke 17:11–19. Money talks, and Jesus makes ours give praise to God.

Sunday between October 23 and 29 inclusive

Joel 2:23–32 (semicontinuous). God fills.

Sunday between October 30 and November 5 inclusive

Isaiah 1:10–18. God launders us, not our money.

Luke 19:1–10. Jesus reorders our homes and unclutters our budgets, making room for salvation.

Sunday between November 6 and 12 inclusive

2 Thessalonians 3:6–13. God sends honest workers and generous givers to show us the way.

Sunday between November 13 and 19 inclusive

Isaiah 65:17–25 (semicontinuous). God promises exiles peace and prosperity.

Notes

Preface

1. Craig A. Satterlee, "Stewardship and Preaching," *Currents in Theology and Mission* 36, no. 5 (October 2009): 350–54.

2. Craig A. Satterlee, "Speaking 'Scripture': We Need Our Own Language to Talk of Faith," *The Lutheran* 23, no. 5 (May 2010): 3.

3. Craig A. Satterlee, *Ambrose of Milan's Method of Mystagogical Preaching* (Collegeville, MN: Liturgical Press, 2002), 12–13, 281–282; Satterlee, *When God Speaks through You: How Faith Convictions Shape Preaching and Mission* (Herndon, VA: Alban Institute, 2007), xxii–xxiii.

Chapter 1: What Do We Mean by Stewardship?

1. John Reumann, *Stewardship and the Economy of God* (Grand Rapids: Wm. B. Eerdmans, 1992), 59.

2. Three of Douglas John Hall's books grew out of an extended engagement with the stewardship movement in North America under the auspices of the Commission for Stewardship of the National Council of Churches of Christ in the USA: *The Steward: A Biblical Symbol Come of Age* (New York: Friendship Press, 1982); *Christian Mission: The Stewardship of Life in the Kingdom of Death* (New York: Friendship Press, 1985); and *Imaging God: Dominion as Stewardship* (Grand Rapids: Eerdmans, 1986).

3. Ronald J. Allen, *Preaching the Topical Sermon* (Louisville, KY: Westminster John Knox Press, 1992), 3.

4. Reumann, *Stewardship and the Economy of God*.

5. Ibid., 115.

6. Phyllis Tickle, *The Great Emergence: How Christianity Is Changing and Why* (Grand Rapids: Baker Books, 2008), 16.

7. Reumann, *Stewardship and the Economy of God*, 2.

8. Allen, *Preaching the Topical Sermon*, 42.

9. James Hudnut-Beumler, *In Pursuit of the Almighty's Dollar: A History of Money* (Chapel Hill: University of North Carolina Press, 2007).

10. Ibid., 64.
11. Ibid., xiii.
12. Ibid., 9.
13. Ibid., 11.
14. Ibid.
15. Ibid., 15.
16. Ibid., 7.
17. Ibid., 45.
18. Craig A. Satterlee, *When God Speaks through Change: Preaching in Times of Congregational Transition* (Herndon, VA: Alban Institute, 2005), 34.

Chapter 2: Why Should We Grow in Giving?

1.   Ronald J. Allen, "Preaching as Mutual Critical Correlation through Conversation," in *Purposes of Preaching*, ed. Jana Childers (St. Louis: Chalice Press, 2004), 10.
2.   Mary Alice Mulligan and Ronald J. Allen, *Make the Word Come Alive: Lessons from Laity* (St. Louis: Chalice Press, 2005), 5.
3.   Craig A. Satterlee, *When God Speaks through Worship: Stories Congregations Live By* (Herndon, VA: Alban Institute, 2009), 114.
4.   Ibid., 115.
5.   Fred B. Craddock, *Preaching* (Nashville: Abingdon Press, 1985), 171.
6.   Ibid., 172.
7.   Martin Luther, "The Small Catechism," *The Book of Concord: The Confessions of the Evangelical Lutheran Church*, ed. Robert Kolb and Timothy K. Wengert (Minneapolis: Fortress Press, 2000), 355.
8.   Jana Childers, "Seeing Jesus: Preaching as Incarnational Act," in Childers, *Purposes of Preaching*, 1.
9.   Mary Donovan Turner, "Disrupting a Ruptured World," in Childers, *Purposes of Preaching*, 135.
10. Bishops' Committee on Priestly Life and Ministry, *Fulfilled in Your Hearing: The Homily in the Sunday Assembly* (Washington, DC: USCCB, 1982), 42, 43. Accessed at http://www.uscb.org/plm/fiyh.pdf.
11. Ibid., 46.
12. Ibid., 47.
13. Walter Brueggemann, *Finally Comes the Poet* (Philadelphia: Fortress Press, 1989), 85.
14. James Hudnut-Beumler, *In Pursuit of the Almighty's Dollar: A History of Money* (Chapel Hill: University of North Carolina Press, 2007), 56–57.
15. Charles L. Campbell, *The Word before the Powers: An Ethic of Preaching* (Louisville, KY: Westminster John Knox Press, 2002), 73.
16. Charles L. Campbell, "Principalities, Powers, and Fools: Does Preaching Make an Ethical Difference," *Homiletic* 33, no. 2 (2008). Accessed at http://

homiletic.net/viewarticle.php?id=6. For a fuller discussion of the foolishness of the Sermon on the Mount, see Charles L. Campbell, "The Folly of the Sermon on the Mount" and "Imagine," in *Preaching the Sermon on the Mount: The World It Imagines,* ed. David Fleer and Dave Bland (St. Louis: Chalice Press, 2007), 59–68, 126–31.

17. Kirsten L. Fryer, "People of Word and Stuff," Lutheran School of Theology at Chicago, March 17, 2009.

18. http://www.mediafamily.org/facts/facts_childadv.shtml.

19. "Facts from *The Story of Stuff,*" http://storyofstuff.com/pdfs/annie_leonard_facts.pdf.

20. Luther, "Small Catechism," *Book of Concord*, 355.

21. Ibid.

Chapter 3: What Does the Bible Say?

1. David L. Bartlett, *Between the Bible and the Church: New Methods for Biblical Preaching* (Nashville: Abingdon Press, 1999), 11.

2. Mark Allan Powell, *Giving to God: The Bible's Good News about Living a Generous Life* (Grand Rapids: Wm. B. Eerdmans, 2006).

3. Ibid., 3–4.

4. Ibid., 4.

5. See, for example, Craig A. Satterlee, *Ambrose of Milan's Method of Mystagogical Preaching* (Collegeville: Liturgical Press, 2002), 322–26; Satterlee, *When God Speaks through Change* (Herndon, VA: Alban Institute, 2005), 47–56; Satterlee, "Patristic Principles for Post-Christendom Preaching," *Liturgy* 25, no. 4 (October–December, 2010): 18–29; Satterlee, "Reflections on Homiletic Method," *Notre Dame Center for Liturgy Bulletin* (February 2008): 4–6.

6. Craig A. Satterlee, *When God Speaks through You: How Faith Convictions Shape Preaching and Mission* (Herndon, VA: Alban Institute, 2007), 167–68.

7. Fred B. Craddock, *Preaching* (Nashville: Abingdon Press, 1985), 99.

8. Ibid., 100.

9. Leonora Tubbs Tisdale, *Prophetic Preaching: A Pastoral Approach* (Louisville, KY: Westminster John Knox Press, 2010), 49–51.

10. Walter Brueggemann, "The Preacher, the Text, and the People," *Theology Today* 47 (1990): 237–47.

11. Satterlee, *When God Speaks through Change*, 34.

Chapter 4: Why Does the Bible Say We Give?

1. Mark Allan Powell, *Giving to God: The Bible's Good News about Living a Generous Life* (Grand Rapids: Wm. B. Eerdmans, 2006), 15.

2.   Craig A. Satterlee, *When God Speaks through You: How Faith Convictions Shape Preaching and Mission* (Herndon, VA: Alban Institute, 2007), 133–48.

3.   Ibid., 24–25.

4.   Walter E. Pilgrim, *Good News for the Poor: Wealth and Poverty in Luke-Acts* (Minneapolis: Augsburg Publishing House, 1981).

5.   Luke 8:1–3; 23:49, 55; 24:1–2, 10, 22; Acts 1:14.

6.   Paul Galbreath, *Leading from the Water* (Herndon, VA: Alban Institute, forthcoming), ch. 2, p. 1.

7.   See Acts 11:29–30; Romans 15:25–27; 1 Corinthians 16:1–4; 2 Corinthians 8–9.

8.   See Galatians 2:6, 9, 11–14. Powell, *Giving to God*, 110.

9.   Timothy V. Olson, "Tithing in a Culture of Affluence," Tithing and Stewardship Foundation, 2008.

10.   Charles L. Campbell, *The Word before the Powers: An Ethic of Preaching* (Louisville, KY: Westminster John Knox Press, 2002), 143.

11.   Ibid.

12.   This sermon was originally published as Craig A. Satterlee, "The Rich Fool," *The Lutheran* 17, no. 6 (June 2004): 24–25.

13.   Powell, *Giving to God*, 10.

14.   Seth Moland-Kovash, "The End of God's Story for You Is Blessing," All Saints Lutheran Church, Palatine, Illinois, November 7, 2010.

15.   Olson, "Tithing in a Culture of Affluence."

16.   Powell, *Giving to God,* 49.

17.   Ibid., 48.

18.   Ibid., 121.

19.   Ibid.

Chapter 5: How Does the Bible Say We Are to Give?

1.   Lutheran Church in America, The American Lutheran Church, The Evangelical Lutheran Church of Canada, and The Lutheran Church—Missouri Synod, *Lutheran Book of Worship* (Minneapolis: Augsburg Publishing House, 1978), 87.

2.   Mark Allan Powell, *Giving to God: The Bible's Good News about Living a Generous Life* (Grand Rapids: Wm. B. Eerdmans, 2006), 52–56.

3.   Comparing preaching and serving a cup of espresso coffee grows out of my research project, "The Preacher and Teacher of Preaching as Barista," which was made possible by a grant from the Wabash Center for Teaching and Learning in Theology and Religion. See http://preaching-and-espresso.blogspot.com/.

4.   Powell, *Giving to God*, 4.

5.   Ibid., 124.

6.   Walter E. Pilgrim, *Good News for the Poor: Wealth and Poverty in Luke-Acts* (Minneapolis: Augsburg Publishing House, 1981), 132–33.

7.   Joel B. Green, *The Gospel of Luke:* The *New International Commentary on the New Testament* (Grand Rapids: Wm. B. Eerdmans, 1997), 672.

8.   Ibid.

9.   James Hudnut-Beumler, *In Pursuit of the Almighty's Dollar: A History of Money* (Chapel Hill: University of North Carolina Press, 2007), 54.

10.   "Giving and Tithing," Christian Broadcasting Network, CBN.com, http://www.cbn.com/spirituallife/CBNTeachingSheets/Giving_And_Tithing.aspx.

Chapter 6: How Much Does the Bible Say We Should Give?

1.   Fidelia H. DeWitt, "Hear the Pennies Dropping," 1890, in *The Sunday School Hymnary* (Great Britain: National Sunday School Union, 1905).

2.   William W. How, "We Give Thee But Thine Own," 1864, in *Cantica Laudis*, by Lowell Mason and George J. Webb (New York: Mason & Law, 1850).

3.   Charles R. Lane, *Ask, Thank, Tell: Improving Stewardship Ministry in Your Congregation* (Minneapolis: Augsburg Fortress, 2006), 21.

4.   James Hudnut-Beumler, *In Pursuit of the Almighty's Dollar: A History of Money* (Chapel Hill: University of North Carolina Press, 2007), 61.

5.   Lane, *Ask, Thank, Tell*, 29.

6.   Mark Allan Powell, *Giving to God: The Bible's Good News about Living a Generous Life* (Grand Rapids: Wm. B. Eerdmans, 2006), 159.

7.   Timothy V. Olson, "Tithing in a Culture of Affluence," Tithing and Stewardship Foundation, 2008.

8.   In the following discussion of the history of tithing, I am indebted to Hudnut-Beumler, *In Pursuit of the Almighty's Dollar*, 52–56.

9.   Powell, *Giving to God*, 157.

10.   Ibid.

11.   Olson, "Tithing in a Culture of Affluence."

12.   Robert Farrar Capon, *Health, Money and Love and Why We Don't Enjoy Them* (Grand Rapids: Wm. B. Eerdmans, 1990), 91.

13.   Powell, *Giving to God*, 160.

14.   Ibid., 158.

15.   See Luke 19:8; Mark 10:21–22; Acts 2:42–45; 4:32.

16.   Powell, *Giving to God*, 140.

17.   Lane, *Ask, Thank, Tell*, 70.

Chapter 7: Why Is This Sermon So Hard?

1.   James R. Nieman and Thomas G. Rogers, *Preaching to Every Pew: Cross-Cultural Strategies* (Minneapolis: Augsburg Fortress, 2001), 60.

2.   Ibid., 58–61.

3.   Charles R. Lane, *Ask, Thank, Tell: Improving Stewardship Ministry in Your Congregation* (Minneapolis: Augsburg Fortress, 2006), 28.

4.   Nieman and Rogers, *Preaching to Every Pew*, 60.

5.   Charles L. Campbell, *The Word before the Powers: An Ethic of Preaching* (Louisville, KY: Westminster John Knox Press, 2002), 2–3.

6.   Donald Perry Kreiss, "No Money, No Mission: Implications for Preaching" (DMin professional paper, Lutheran School of Theology at Chicago, 2007), 44.

7.   Ibid., 83.

8.   Ibid., 80–81.

9.   Nieman and Rogers, *Preaching to Every Pew*, 65–67.

10. Ibid., 69–73.

11. James Hudnut-Beumler, *In Pursuit of the Almighty's Dollar: A History of Money* (Chapel Hill: University of North Carolina Press, 2007), 94–96.

12. Joseph R. Jeter Jr. and Ronald J. Allen, *One Gospel, Many Ears: Preaching for Different Listeners in the Congregation* (St. Louis: Chalice Press, 2002), 22.

13. T. A. Kantonen, *A Theology for Christian Stewardship* (Philadelphia: Muhlenberg, 1956), 24.

14. Walter E. Pilgrim, *Good News for the Poor: Wealth and Poverty in Luke-Acts* (Minneapolis: Augsburg Publishing House, 1981), 124.

15. See Luke 5:29; 7:1–10, 36–50; 14:1, 15–24; 15:11–24; 16:25; 19:1; 22:18; 23:50.

16. Mark Allan Powell, *Giving to God: The Bible's Good News about Living a Generous Life* (Grand Rapids: Wm. B. Eerdmans, 2006), 86.

17. Ibid., 119.

18. Ibid., 138.

19. Ibid.

20. Ibid., 139.

21. Hudnut-Beumler, *In Search of the Almighty's Dollar*, 72.

22. Ibid., 75.

23. Ibid.

24. Ibid., 217.

25. See Craig A. Satterlee, *When God Speaks through You: How Faith Convictions Shape Preaching and Mission* (Herndon, VA: Alban Institute, 2007), 25–37.

26. Ronald A. Heifetz, *Leadership without Easy Answers* (Cambridge, MA: Belknap Press, 1994), 22, 87.

27. Leonora Tubbs Tisdale, *Prophetic Preaching: A Pastoral Approach* (Louisville, KY: Westminster John Knox Press, 2010), 60.

28. O. Wesley Allen Jr., *The Homiletic of All Believers: A Conversational Approach to Proclamation and Preaching* (Louisville, KY: Westminster John Knox Press, 2005), 57.

Chapter 8: What Else Can We Do?

1.   Charles R. Lane, *Ask, Thank, Tell: Improving Stewardship Ministry in Your Congregation* (Minneapolis: Augsburg Fortress, 2006), 67.

2.   James Hudnut-Beumler, *In Pursuit of the Almighty's Dollar: A History of Money* (Chapel Hill: University of North Carolina Press, 2007), 157.

3.   Ibid., 63.

4.   Hudnut-Beumler, *In Pursuit of the Almighty's Dollar*, 159.

5.   Lane, *Ask, Thank, Tell*, 77–78.

6.   Craig A. Satterlee, *When God Speaks through You: How Faith Convictions Shape Preaching and Mission* (Herndon, VA: Alban Institute, 2007), 69–71.

7.   Anna Carter Florence, *Preaching as Testimony* (Louisville, KY: Westminster John Knox Press, 2007), xx.

8.   Lane, *Ask, Thank, Tell*, 69.

9.   Satterlee, *When God Speaks through You*, 168–72.

10.   Hudnut-Beumler, *In Pursuit of the Almighty's Dollar*, 156.

11.   Lane, *Ask, Thank, Tell*, 13.

12.   Hudnut-Beumler, *In Pursuit of the Almighty's Dollar*, 157.

13.   Lane, *Ask, Thank, Tell*, 77.

14.   David J. Schlafer, *What Makes This Day Different? Preaching Grace on Special Occasions* (Boston: Cowley Publications, 1998), 17–21.

15.   Ibid., 18.

16.   Lutheran Church in America, The American Lutheran Church, The Evangelical Lutheran Church of Canada, The Lutheran Church—Missouri Synod, *Lutheran Book of Worship: Ministers Desk Edition* (Minneapolis: Augsburg Publishing House, 1978), 28, nos. 24–25.

17.   Ibid.

18.   Jonathan Linman, *Holy Conversation: Spirituality for Worship* (Minneapolis: Fortress Press, 2010), 125.

19.   Ibid.

20.   Evangelical Lutheran Church in America, *Evangelical Lutheran Worship: Leaders Desk Edition* (Minneapolis: Augsburg Fortress, 2006), 21.

21.   Lorraine S. Brugh and Gordon W. Lathrop, *The Sunday Assembly* (Minneapolis: Augsburg Fortress, 2008), 177.

22.   Ibid.

23.   Ibid., 195.

24.   Ibid.

25.   Ibid.

26.   Hudnut-Beumler, *In Pursuit of the Almighty's Dollar*, 55–56.

27.   Gordon W. Lathrop, "Justin, Eucharist, and 'Sacrifice': A Case of Metaphor," *Worship* 64, no. 1 (January 1990): 30–48.

28.   Ibid., 31.

29.   Ibid., 32.

30.   William Seth Adams, *Shaped by Images: One Who Presides* (New York: Church Hymnal Corporation, 1995), 89.

31.   Ibid.

32.   Mark P. Bangert, "Liturgy and Stewardship," *Currents in Theology and Mission* 36, no. 5 (October 2009): 345.

33.   Craig A. Satterlee, *Ambrose of Milan's Method of Mystagogical Preaching* (Collegeville, MN: Liturgical Press, 2002), 180–81.

34.   For more on teaching following participation, see Craig A. Satterlee, *When God Speaks through Worship: Stories Congregations Live By* (Herndon, VA: Alban Institute, 2009), 17–30.

35.   Edward Yarnold, SJ, *The Awe-Inspiring Rites of Initiation: The Origins of the R.C.I.A.*, 2nd ed. (Collegeville, MN: Liturgical Press, 1994), 40.

36.   Ibid.

37.   Ibid., 42.

38. Edward J. Kilmartin, SJ, "The Sacrifice of Thanksgiving and Social Justice," in *Liturgy and Social Justice*, ed. Mark Searle (Collegeville: Liturgical Press, 1980), 54.

39. Adams, *Shaped By Images*, 89

Afterword

1.   Cyril of Jerusalem, "Sermon 1: The Prebaptismal Rites," no. 3, in Edward Yarnold, SJ, *The Awe-Inspiring Rites of Initiation: The Origins of the R.C.I.A.*, 2nd ed. (Collegeville, MN: Liturgical Press, 1994), 71.

2.   Ibid., 39.